DRAWING
on the
POWERS
of
HEAVEN

Grant Von Harrison

DRAWING
on the
POWERS
of
HEAVEN

Keepsake Paperbacks
Orem, Utah

Missionary Success Series (books and tapes)
Tools for Missionaries
Tools for Missionaries - Trainer's Manual
Converting Thousands
Serve the Lord with Your Heart
Every Missionary Can Baptize
Teaching with Power
Missionaries Need to Know God
Converting with the Book of Mormon
Conversion Power of the Book of Mormon
The Doctrine of the Discussions

Personal Enrichment Series (books and tapes)
Drawing on the Powers of Heaven
Drawing on the Powers of Heaven - Spanish
Understanding Your Divine Nature
Seeing with an Eye of Faith
Is Kissing Sinful?
Fathers as Patriarchs
As a Man Speaketh, So Is He
Do You Know God?

Contents

Foreword

The insights represented in this book were acquired by the author to a great extent while he was serving as a missionary. He has a deep sense of gratitude for these insights, and senses very keenly the profound influence they have had on his life. For this reason, all personal revenues realized from the sale of this book will be used to support missionary work.

The author requests that if the reader feels his life is significantly blessed as a result of this book he will make an additional donation to the Missionary Department of the Church of Jesus Christ of Latter-day Saints. This can be done by check or money order made payable to the L.D.S. Church and mailed to:

Missionary Department
Church Office Building
50 East North Temple
Salt Lake City, Utah 84150

Preface

The following statement by Elder Bruce R. McConkie refers to a process with which every member of the Church of Jesus Christ of Latter-day Saints should be conversant. Referring to the process of prayer, he encourages us to "learn how to [pray] boldly and efficaciously, not in word only but in spirit and in power, *so that we may pull upon ourselves . . . the very powers of heaven.*"[1]

The powers of heaven are very real and can dramatically influence the course of events in a person's life. In our relationship with Diety, the powers of heaven include any influence or power (inspiration, gift of the spirit, power of the priesthood, etc.) which is governed by God and operates in our behalf. A study of the scriptures reveals that the ways the powers of heaven can assist mortal men are virtually unlimited.

To realize your ultimate potential in this mortal life, you must learn to draw upon the powers of heaven. No amount of knowledge or skill can compensate for the absence of the powers of heaven in your life. With the powers of heaven to

---

[1] Bruce R. McConkie, "Why the Lord Ordained Prayer," *The Ensign*, January 1976, p. 9, italics added.

assist you, you can be successful in this mortal life in spite of weaknesses because, in a very literal sense, the powers of heaven compensate for human weaknesses. If you learn to call down the powers of heaven, your limitations—background and physical characteristics—become insignificant. The Lord has promised if you come unto him in humility with sufficient faith, your weaknesses will become strengths:

> And if men come unto me I will show unto them their weakness. I give unto men weakness that they may be humble; and my grace is sufficient for all men that humble themselves before me; for *if they humble themselves before me, and have faith in me, then will I make weak things become strong unto them.* (Ether 12:27, italics added.)

Our access to the powers of heaven makes this promise possible. If you learn to pull down the powers of heaven upon yourself, your talents and abilities will be greatly magnified. Your ultimate achievements in this life will be determined more by your ability to pull down the powers of heaven upon yourself than reliance on your natural abilities. President Ezra Taft Benson has said:

> Men and women who turn their lives over to God will find out that he can make a lot more out of their lives than they can. He will deepen their joys, expand their vision, quicken their minds, strengthen their muscles, lift their spirits, multiply their blessings, increase their opportunities, comfort their souls, raise up friends, and pour out peace. Whoever will lose his life to God will find he has eternal life.[2]

When you learn to draw on the powers of heaven, you will see this promise fulfilled in your life.

The powers of heaven are governed by spiritual laws; their receipt is always predicated upon obedience to law. When you understand and learn to comply with these laws, you will be able to consistently call upon the powers of heaven to assist you in your endeavors. The scriptures tell us very clearly that we must be obedient to specific laws in order to receive blessings from God.

---

[2]Ezra Taft Benson, "Jesus Christ, Gifts and Expectations," *The New Era*, May 1975, p. 20.

There is a law, irrevocably decreed in heaven before the foundations of this world, upon which all blessings are predicated—And when we obtain any blessing from God, it is by obedience to that law upon which it is predicated. (D&C 130:20-21.)

It is through your own efforts that you qualify for the various endowments and blessings that come through the powers of heaven.

...the powers of heaven cannot be controlled nor handled only upon the principles of righteousness. (D&C 121:36.)

Once you realize that the powers of heaven are governed by law, the challenge is to become conversant with those laws and principles that govern the powers of heaven. It is very difficult, if not impossible, to be obedient to given laws or principles unless you know what those laws are and have a clear understanding of what is required to comply with them.

When you finish reading this book, you will have a clear understanding of faith in general, but most importantly, you will have a clear understanding of the processes of faith that govern the powers of heaven. You will know very specifically how to draw on the powers of heaven to assist you in achieving your righteous desires. You will understand the role of the thought process in exercising faith and how to cope with the trials of faith you can expect to encounter as you do, in fact, attempt to draw upon the powers of heaven.

Unfortunately, many members of the Church are limited in all aspects of their mortal endeavors (church assignments, parental and professional responsibilities, social life, schooling, etc.) because they do not know how to call down the powers of heaven in their own behalf. The express purpose of this book is to teach members of the Church how to call down the powers of heaven. In order to tap heavenly powers, a person must know how to exercise faith because the powers of heaven are governed by faith.

As you read this book you will come to the realization that there is much more to the process of exercising faith than you had realized. At this point in your life your understanding of faith is most likely based upon this familiar definition of faith.

> Now faith is the substance of things hoped for, the evidence of things not seen. (Hebrews 11:1.)

A person's ability to draw on the powers of heaven is extremely limited unless he understands very specifically the process required to exercise faith. The ability to state a vague definition of faith is not sufficient.

Exercising the faith required to call upon the powers of heaven involves a very specific process. In order to be proficient at exercising faith, you must understand the process thoroughly and then learn to apply the process in your daily pursuits. This book will help you understand the process required to pull down the powers of heaven to bless your life. When you successfully follow this process, you will be able to call upon the powers of heaven to assist you in realizing your righteous desires.

Even though faith is a gift of God, we obtain it only by exercising our agency. It is essential that you understand that you increase and perfect your faith by exercising your agency. (see Orson Pratt's "True Faith," in *Lectures on Faith*.) This book is intended to assist you in your effort to increase and perfect your faith.

Chapter One

The Nature and Function of Faith

G enerally, members of the Church do not have difficulty understanding the most basic aspects of faith,
such as faith that God lives, that Jesus is the Christ,
that there is life after death, or with a general faith in the
overall plan of salvation. However, many people do have
trouble understanding the specific kind of faith required to
draw on the powers of heaven to help them be more successful
in every facet in their lives.

Regarding faith, the Prophet Joseph Smith taught that:
1) "...as faith is *the moving cause of all action* in temporal
concerns, so it is in spiritual;" 2) "...faith is not only the
principle of action, *but of power also,*" and 3) "Faith, then, is
the first great governing principle which has power,
dominion, and authority over *all* things."³

If you think about it, it is easy to see that faith is the
moving cause of all action—exercising, planting a garden,
studying for an examination. However, many members of the
Church have trouble understanding the process required to

³ Joseph Smith, *Lectures on Faith* (S.L.C.: N. B. Lundwall), pp. 8 & 10, italics added.

1

experience what Joseph Smith referred to as the power that comes through faith. It is important that members of the Church understand that this power comes from God and learn to call upon this power, because without the powers of heaven we are extremely limited in what we can accomplish in all aspects of our lives. Members of the Church have "power given them to do all things by faith." (2 Nephi 1:10.) By means of faith as a principle of power, people accomplish or experience things they could not otherwise accomplish or experience.

The Function of Faith

The following example illustrates the role of faith in motivating a person to action.

> If a man desires to lose 10 lbs., he must take the following steps:
> 1. Have faith in the laws that determine weight loss.
> 2. Make a resolve to exercise daily and eat less.
> 3. Maintain a constant effort, motivated by faith.

Many desires, however, cannot be realized by the faith that motivates us to action alone. There are many desires that require specific help from the Lord, in addition to resolve and determination on our part. For instance, if a man becomes lost while hunting during a heavy snow storm and he begins to pray that the Lord will preserve his life by inspiring him as to what direction he should go to find shelter or help, this desire will not be realized unless he is successful in calling down the powers of heaven to assist him.

Faith, then, as a principle of action involves resolve, decision-making, and determination. Faith as a principle of power involves resolve, decision-making, determination, plus: 1) Belief in the Lord Jesus Christ, 2) determination on the part of the individual to respond to the requirements of God, and 3) bestowal of the powers of heaven (added strength, power, and force from God himself).

Many righteous desires are very personal in nature and should be pursued through individual faith. However, there are some desires that warrant or require the collective faith of more than one person. When this is the case, you need to be very mindful of the faith, or lack of faith, of others. In some instances, the lack of faith on the part of the majority will stifle the faith of a righteous minority. In other words, under some conditions righteous desires will not be realized even if there are some with sufficient faith to release the powers of heaven.

Throughout the scriptures we see how the faith of the individual results in blessings for the masses. From the scriptures we also learn, however, that there are exceptions to this. For example, when Mormon was called upon to be the military leader for the Nephites, his faith was a key factor in their success in battle. Yet the Nephites failed to see the hand of the Lord in their success and boasted of their own strength. Finally, Mormon's ability to exercise faith in their behalf was stifled.

> Behold, I had led them, notwithstanding their wickedness I had led them many times to battle, and had loved them, according to the love of God which was in me, with all my heart; and my soul had been poured out in prayer unto my God all the day long for them; nevertheless, it was without faith, because of the hardness of their hearts. (Mormon 3:12.)

There are indeed many instances where the influence of the powers of heaven require collective faith. In the case of missionary work, the lack of faith of one companion can curtail the influence of the Spirit when the missionaries are trying to teach a family. Likewise, the lack of faith on the part of several people can curtail the Spirit in a church meeting.

An individual (missionary, ward leader, etc.) with great faith can draw upon the powers of heaven, but the process is facilitated when more than one person lends faith to the same desired ends.

When someone is ill, the composite faith of all of those associated with the blessing govern the powers of heaven. Obviously, great faith on the part of one person can have a tremendous effect when someone receives a blessing, but in the final analysis, it is the combined faith, or lack of faith, of everyone associated with the blessing that determines whether or not the blessing is realized.

Once you become proficient at calling down the powers of heaven through faith, you should make every effort to teach others the process. If you work at it diligently, you will realize that you can be instrumental in teaching many others to be effective in calling down the powers of heaven. You will find that once others with whom you associate learn to exercise faith, the endeavors of the group will be sustained by the powers of heaven to a phenomenal degree.

In missions, stakes, wards, and families, etc. where groups begin to exercise collective faith, the outpourings of the powers of heaven result in the lives of thousands of people being blessed. The most obvious indicator of collective faith is the number of people joining the Church in a given area. Collective faith is the key to the realization of President Kimball's desire to see millions of people join the Church each year. Once the collective faith of the Church is sufficient, millions will join the Church each year, and the prophecies referring to the Church rolling forth as a stone and encompassing the entire earth will be fulfilled. As members of the Church, we need to realize that the fulfillment of these prophecies is contingent on the collective faith of the members of the Church. You will find it much easier to exercise faith when your faith is sustained by the faith of others, as is the case with many physical tasks (e.g., lifting heavy objects, pushing a car) which cannot be accomplished unless people combine their physical strength. So it is with many righteous desires; they require the collective or combined faith of many people.

The following diagram depicts the process when someone is converted through the power of faith and prayer.

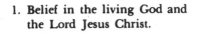

1. Belief in the living God and the Lord Jesus Christ.

2. Plus determination to respond to the requirements of God. (Righteous living, following the counsel of the Prophet, friendshipping the person, etc.)

3. Faith in the power from God at your disposal.

THOSE CONCERNED WITH THE CONVERSION OF THE PERSON

PERSON RECEIVING THE GOSPEL

The first time you read this book answer the following questions on a piece of paper.

Explain what is meant by the "powers of heaven."

How does the faith required to lose 10 lbs. differ from the faith required to see someone converted through the power of faith and prayer?

If possible, discuss your answers with someone else who is reading this book.

Chapter Two

Faith
and the Powers of Heaven

Once you develop a basic faith in the overall plan of salvation, repent, acquire a testimony of the restored gospel, and live in harmony with the gospel, you are in a position to exercise the faith that unlocks the powers of heaven. With these powers you will be able to accomplish righteous desires that require the Lord's help, such as securing a good job, overcoming a bad habit, seeing someone converted, or speaking with the power of the Holy Ghost when you give a talk.

Unless you exercise sufficient faith, you deny the Lord the opportunity to help you in the course of your daily life. The scriptures teach us that certain powers of heaven are governed by the faith of mortal men:

> And neither at any time hath any wrought miracles *until after their faith.* (Ether 12:18, italics added.)

> The Lord is able to do all things according to his will, for the children of men, *if it so be that they exercise faith in him.* (I Nephi 7:12, italics added.)

> Deny not the power of God; for he worketh by power, *according to the faith of the children of men.* (Moroni 10:7, italics added.)

> For behold, I am God; and I am a God of miracles... and *I work not among the children of men save it be according to their faith*. (2 Nephi 27:23, italics added.)
>
> And Christ hath said: If ye will have faith in me ye shall have power to do whatsoever thing is expedient in me. (Moroni 7:33)
>
> Remember that *without faith you can do nothing*. (D&C 8:10, italics added.)

Moroni thoroughly understood the role of faith in releasing the powers of heaven. This is evident in his response to a revelation he received regarding his ability to overcome his weaknesses. (Ether 12:27.) He made the following statements when he expressed his gratitude to the Lord:

> And I, Moroni, having heard these words, was comforted, and said: O Lord, thy righteous will be done, for I know that thou workest unto the children of men according to their faith;... For thus didst thou manifest thyself unto thy disciples; for after they had faith, and did speak in thy name, thou didst show thyself unto them in great power. (Ether 12:29, 31.)

Jesus performed miracles according to the faith of the people as shown in the following scriptures: Matthew 8:13, 9:20-22; 13:58; 3 Nephi 17:8.

It is important that you understand that the influence of the powers of heaven in your life is governed or controlled by faith. In other words, the Lord's hands are tied until you exercise faith. Just as faith without works is dead (James 2:14-20), works without faith are dead since they are not sustained by the powers of heaven. The Lord has said that if we have fears (doubts) in our hearts, we deny ourselves the blessings of heaven. (D&C 67:3.) For example, if you lack faith, you may spend hours preparing to teach a Sunday School lesson and still not be effective in touching the hearts of the members of your class. No matter how much time you devote to a task, your ultimate level of achievement is limited unless you learn to exercise the faith required to release the added strength and power from God that is at your disposal.

I would estimate of those members of the Church who are motivated to pay a full tithing, there are significant numbers who in turn, deny themselves the full blessings that come from the payment of tithes because they fail to exercise faith sufficient to allow the Lord to bless them for obedience to the law of tithing. You must realize that the payment of tithing is compliance with only part of the law. The full law requires us to have faith that makes it possible for the Lord to bless us for paying our tithes. The same principle holds true when we administer to the sick. The Lord does not bless the person beyond the combined faith of those associated with the administration. Certainly there are many blessings the Lord would like to extend to individual members of the Church if they would merely exercise the faith that would allow him to extend the blessings. In other words, our righteous living (works) generally exceeds our faith. If our faith were greater, we would realize many more blessings which the Lord wishes us to have and for which we have qualified as a result of our righteous living.

The process of raising crops provides an excellent example of faith as a motivation of action which under some conditions, requires us to call on the powers of heaven for assistance. Let's analyze this process. Your faith in the process of life motivates you to plant seeds, water crops, etc. However, if the crops are threatened by a natural calamity such as drought—or, as in the early days of the Church, by crickets— you may find it necessary to call upon the powers of heaven to preserve your crops.

Let's consider a missionary faced with the task of memorizing the missionary discussions. Faith will give him the assurance that he can memorize the discussions if he applies himself to the task. If he relies on the faith that motivates him to action exclusively, the time it takes him to memorize the discussions will be determined by his ability. If he exercises the faith necessary to call down the powers of heaven, however, his ability to memorize will be facilitated through the Spirit and he will be able to memorize the discussions in much less time.

The role of faith to motivate, as well as the power that can come through faith, applies to all learning. Through the powers of heaven our intellectual abilities can be magnified. In addition, the Lord has said we can be taught from on high if we seek specific knowledge by means of "the prayer of faith." (D&C 52:9.) Through the powers of heaven, insights and understandings can be revealed to our minds. This promise applies to all areas of inquiry, not just theology. For example, if parents are having difficulty coping with certain behavioral problems of a child, they can be taught through inspiration how to cope with the child's problem.

Let's analyze the role of faith in inspiration. If a person is faced with a difficult decision, faith can motivate that person to pray and seek guidance from his Father in Heaven. However, unless he exercises the faith required to call down the powers of heaven, the Lord cannot inspire him regarding his problem. In other words, the individual's faith governs to a great extent his ability to receive inspiration.

Another example is the effort of a Latter-day Saint to prompt a nonmember to join the Church. Faith can motivate the person to spend time with the nonmember and fellowship him in all outward respects. Through the power of faith the Church member can request that the nonmember be touched by the Spirit so the nonmember will be prompted to investigate the gospel.

In each of these examples it is easy to see the role of faith in motivating an individual to action and the role of faith as a principle of power in drawing on the powers of heaven. In the future you should make a special effort to analyze the role of faith in your endeavors. You should make a conscious effort to analyze the role of faith in motivating you to action and instances when the situation requires faith as a principle of power. By doing so you will become much more aware of faith as a principle of power.

In summary, you should consistently call upon the Lord to assist you in achieving righteous desires and then make certain that faith accompanies your righteous living, thereby allowing the Lord the opportunity to bless you.

The first time you read this book answer the following question on a piece of paper.

What governs the powers of heaven as they relate to the achievement of righteous desires?

If possible, discuss your answer with someone else who is reading this book.

Faith—The Key to Excellence

In the course of your life there are many things required of you that you cannot accomplish to a degree of excellence without the Lord's help. There will be many things you will do every day that you could do much better if you knew how to call down the powers of heaven to assist you. In order to realize your full potential, you must learn to exercise abiding faith that the Lord will help you achieve goals and expectations that you cannot achieve without the Lord's help. Exercising such faith involves a very specific process which has to be both learned and mastered.

Righteousness—A Prerequisite to Faith

Unless your life is in harmony with the basic tenets of the gospel (e.g., purity of thought and action, proper motives, obedience, dedication) you will not be able to exercise faith that will release the powers of heaven. (see Mormon 1:13-14.) The Lord has stipulated "that the powers of heaven cannot be controlled nor handled only upon principles of righteousness." (D&C 121:36.) When you are keeping the Lord's commandments (e.g. paying a full tithe, studying the gospel, carrying out your church assignments conscientiously, refraining from inappropriate conversations) you will be able to pull down the powers of heaven to bless your life.

I, the Lord, am bound when ye do what I say; but when ye do not what I say, ye have no promise. (D&C 82:10.)

Bruce R. McConkie tells us that *"Faith is a gift of God bestowed as a reward for personal righteousness.* It is always given when righteousness is present, and the greater the measure of obedience to God's laws the greater will be the endowment of faith."[4] Consequently, faith as a principle of power can only be exercised by those who conform to the principles of truth that come from God.

If you can answer the following questions in the affirmative you can be assured your life is sufficiently in harmony with gospel principles to exercise faith as a principle of power.

1. If you have ever been involved in a transgression relating to the law of chastity, was it resolved by the proper priesthood authority?

2. Do you earnestly strive to do your duty in the Church by attending Priesthood Meeting, Sacrament Meeting, etc.?

3. Do you sustain the President of the Church as Prophet, Seer, and Revelator, recognizing that no other man on earth holds all the priesthood keys?

4. Do you sustain the other local and general authorities of the Church?

5. Do you pay a full tithing?

6. Are you totally honest in your dealings with your fellow men?

7. Do you live the Word of Wisdom?

8. Do you earnestly try to live in accordance with all of the accepted rules and doctrines of the Church?

9. Do you read the scriptures on a regular basis?

10. Do you refrain from conversations that would offend the Lord?

11. If there has been anything amiss in your life, was it resolved with the proper priesthood authorities?

With regard to your personal worthiness, you should be aware of the seriousness of lying to one of the Lord's representatives or failing to live up to promises made to them. The Lord will not tolerate misrepresentation to one of his desig-

---

[4] Bruce R. McConkie, *Mormon Doctrine* (S.L.C.: Bookcraft, 1966), p. 264, italics in original.

nated representatives. President Kimball has warned that "those who lie to Church leaders forget or ignore an important rule and truth the Lord has set down: that when he has called men to high places in his kingdom and has placed on them the mantle of authority, a lie to them is tantamount to a lie to the Lord; a half-truth to his officials is like a half-truth to the Lord."[5] The Lord will not be mocked. If you feel you need further clarification regarding confession to one of the Lord's anointed, read President Kimball's book, *The Miracle of Forgiveness.*

The first time you read this book answer the following question on a piece of paper.

Who can exercise faith as a principle of power?

If possible, discuss your answer with someone else who is reading this book.

Righteous Desires and Faith

The Lord has promised He will grant unto men according to their desires:

I know that he [the Lord] granteth unto men according to their desire. (Alma 29:4.)

Verily, verily, I say unto you, even as you desire of me so it shall be done unto you. (D&C 11:8.)

Desire is more than a mere wish—it is a motivating conviction that moves one to action. The following excerpts from a talk given by Elder Bruce R. McConkie to new mission presidents provides additional insight into the relationship between desire and faith:

Baptizing is a matter of attitude, desire and feeling. We want converts, and we never say to a missionary, "Don't baptize unless." We always say: "You can baptize; there are choice, wonderful people out there; and here is how you do it." We give them an intelligent,

---

[5] Spencer W. Kimball, *The Miracle of Forgiveness* (S.L.C.: Bookcraft, 1969), p. 183.

affirmative approach; we instruct them in how to do it; and we motivate them. Then somehow or other the Lord does the rest, and they get people into the Church. "If thou canst believe, all things are possible to him that believeth." (Mark 9:23.)

We have to ask the Lord for help; we have to seek converts; we have to desire baptisms; we have to know that we receive according to our desires, and if we desire to get such and such a thing, and have faith in the Lord, it is going to eventuate.

We are not getting the results that we ought to get. We are not getting the number of baptisms that in my judgment the Lord expects us to get. To a degree, at least, we are grinding our wheels without going forward....

Perhaps what is wrong is that we have not desired in faith with all our hearts to bring souls into the kingdom. Perhaps we have not made up our minds that we can and will bring people into the Church.

Now, very frankly, whether we gain many converts or few depends in large measure upon our frame of mind.[6]

We see an example of what Elder McConkie is talking about in the missionary labors of Alma. In the eighth year of the reign of the judges, Alma was the chief judge as well as the high priest (president) of the Church. The Church began to fail in its progress because the people began to be lifted up in their pride, to set their hearts upon riches and upon the vain things of the world. In an effort to correct the situation, Alma appointed someone else chief judge over the people so he could devote his time exclusively to the ministry.

Alma's strong desire to see people join the Church becomes very evident when the people in the city of Ammonihah reject his message. When Alma first attempted to preach to the people in Ammonihah, they would not listen because Satan had a great hold on their hearts. But Alma still desired to see them baptized. He prayed that the way would be prepared so that he could baptize them. The record says that he "labored much in the spirit, wrestling with God in mighty prayer, that he would pour out his Spirit upon the people

---

[6] Bruce R. McConkie, Mission President Seminar, June 21, 1975, pp. 1-4.

who were in the city; that he would also grant that he might baptize them unto repentance." (Alma 8:10.)

Then, according to Alma's desire, the Lord prepared the way for the baptism of a very prominent and wealthy man, Amulek, his wife, his children, and his kinsfolk. (Alma 10:11.)

Following his conversion, Amulek joins Alma in the ministry with the result that many people in Ammonihah "began to repent, and to search the scriptures." (Alma 14:1.) Amulek continued to assist Alma in the ministry over the next several years, "and the establishment of the church became general throughout the land, in all the region round about, among all the people of the Nephites." (Alma 16:15.)

From Alma's account of his missionary labors, it is obvious that Amulek played a very important role in the establishment of the Church throughout the land. It appears that Alma's ultimate success in seeing thousands baptized would never have been realized if he had not desired with all his heart to baptize the people in Ammonihah even after they had rejected his message.

Later, when Alma undertook a mission to the Zoramites, he again prayed for success.

> O Lord, wilt thou comfort my soul, and give unto me success,... O Lord, wilt thou grant unto us that we may have success in bringing them again unto thee in Christ. (Alma 31:32 & 34.)

Once again he convinced the Lord he was willing to pay any price to succeed.

> O Lord, wilt thou give me strength, that I may bear with mine infirmities.... O Lord, wilt thou grant unto me that I may have strength, that I may suffer with patience these afflictions which shall come upon me. (Alma 31:30-31.)

And again, the Lord granted according to his desires and gave him success in his labors.

We see this same pattern in the missionary labors of Ammon, one of the sons of Mosiah. Ammon's desire resulted in the conversion of a very influential man (King Lamoni), the way was opened and thousands were baptized. It is important to realize that Ammon was not successful in his missionary labors until his desires had motivated him to be patient and long-suffering in his afflictions. He had experienced many afflictions. He had suffered much, both in body and in mind, with hunger, thirst, and fatigue. Just as Alma had, so did Ammon "labor in the spirit." (Alma 17:5.)

In other words, he had to convince the Lord he wanted to baptize the Lamanites and was willing to pay any price in order to succeed; and then "the Lord... granted unto [him] according to [his] prayers." (Alma 25:17.)

Modern day missionaries will be much more successful in their labors if they will heed Elder McConkie's counsel:

> Perhaps what is wrong is that we have not desired in faith with all our hearts to bring souls into the kingdom. Perhaps we have not made up our minds that we can bring people into the Church.[7]

If missionaries cultivate a sincere desire to baptize people, and convince the Lord they are willing to pay any price in terms of hard work, etc., the Lord will grant their desires and they will be instrumental in baptizing people.

What Elder McConkie says regarding desire in the context of missionary work applies to all righteous desires. If you are not realizing your desires, you are not desiring in faith with all your heart; consequently the Lord cannot assist you in realizing your righteous desires. Remember, you will receive according to your desires. As Elder McConkie said, "If we desire to get such and such a thing, and have faith in the Lord, it is going to eventuate."[8] If you set a goal to achieve a particular righteous desire and then find you lack initiative in pursuing the goal, you must conclude the goal is not a true desire. If it were a true desire, you would be motivated to action. Many people will say in passing that they would give anything if they could play the piano well. Yet, in reality,

[7]Bruce R. McConkie, Ibid.
[8]Bruce R. McConkie, Ibid.

they would never pay the price of practicing every day for years to perfect the talent. If you truly desire something, you will have the necessary motivation to pursue your goal thoroughly. By contrast, if your goal is not a sincere desire, you will not be inclined to pay the price required to achieve it.

Attitudes and desires are formed as a direct result of what we think about. When a person chooses not to use his free will in directing his thoughts, he leaves the dimensions of the mind that control his desires wide open to suggestion. If we do not make an exerted effort to control and direct our thinking, our desires and attitudes will be influenced primarily by the adversary, other people, music, movies, T.V., radio, newspapers, etc. So you have the choice of deliberately directing your thinking, or allowing other forces to dictate your desires and attitudes.

We are responsible for our thoughts. Consequently, as individuals, we are responsible for our attitudes and desires because our thoughts govern our inner desires. We are ambitious or lazy, interesting or dull, faithful or disobedient, dependable or undependable, successful or unsuccessful according to our attitudes and desires. And frankly, whether we realize many righteous desires or few is dependent in large measure on our frame of mind. Therefore, it is important that we learn to control our thoughts and focus on righteous desires.

The first time you read this book answer the following questions on a piece of paper.

What is desire?

According to Elder McConkie, what must missionaries do in order to have more success in bringing people into the Church?

Explain how lack of desire and faith account for failure in other aspects of life.

If possible, discuss your answers with someone else who is reading this book.

Chapter Three

The Principles that Govern Faith

I. Selecting Righteous Desires

In order to draw on the powers of heaven, you must systematically decide what you want the Lord to help you accomplish. It is impossible to exercise faith in the powers of heaven at your disposal without having a very specific end in mind. The most serious failing on the part of most members of the Church with respect to faith as a principle of power is their failure to make specific decisions regarding things they want the Lord to assist them with. For example, unless you systematically make the decision that you want to be instrumental in someone's conversion, the prospect that you will play a part in someone's conversion is quite remote.

> Behold, I say unto you that whoso believeth in Christ, doubting nothing, whatsoever he shall ask the Father in the name of Christ it shall be granted him; and this promise is unto all, even unto the ends of the earth. (Mormon 9:21.)

In your dealings with the Lord, the need to ask for specific blessings is an absolute requirement. Dedication alone is not sufficient. You must request blessings.

> Therefore, if you will ask of me you shall receive; if you will knock
> it shall be opened unto you. (D&C 11:5.)

This same promise is reiterated at least one hundred times throughout the scriptures; however, you cannot take advantage of this promise unless you are willing to ask the Lord in faith to help you achieve your desires.

> I can promise you that the spirit is a whole lot more anxious to
> help you than you are to be helped.[9]

If we realized blessings as a direct result of dedication, we would lose sight of the hand of the Lord in the blessings we received. It is for this reason the Lord has stipulated we must *ask* in order to receive blessings.

You have the responsibility to make certain that your righteous desires are properly focused. The Lord has said:

> Remember that without faith you can do nothing; therefore ask in
> faith. Trifle not with these things; *do not ask for that which you ought
> not.* (D&C 8:10, italics added.)

> Whatsoever ye ask the Father in my name it shall be given unto
> you, *that is expedient for you; And if ye ask anything that is not
> expedient for you, it shall turn unto your condemnation.* (D&C
> 88:64-65, italics added.)

> And now, if God, who has created you, on whom you are
> dependent for your lives and for all that ye have and are, *doth grant
> unto you whatsoever ye ask that is right, in faith, believing that ye shall
> recieve,* O then, how ye ought to impart of the substance that ye have
> one to another. (Mosiah 4:21, italics added.)

> And now, because thou hast done this with such unwearyingness,
> behold, I will bless thee forever; and I will make thee mighty in word
> and in deed, in faith and in works; yea, even that all things shall be
> done unto thee according to thy word, *for thou shalt not ask that which
> is contrary to my will.* (Helaman 10:5, italics added.)

> . . . ye must not perform any thing unto the Lord save in the first
> place ye shall pray unto the Father in the name of Christ, that he will
> consecrate thy performance unto thee, that thy performance may be for
> the welfare of thy soul. (2 Nephi 32:9.)

---

[9] S. Dilworth Young, talk given in the Missionary Home, June 1975.

Pure motives are prerequisite to the ability to call down the powers of heaven. The Lord will not sustain your efforts to achieve, excel, or receive special blessings if your desires are vain. (See Galations 5:26.) However, you should realize that you can have an eye single to the glory of God and still desire to excel in athletics, school, your vocation, etc. An eye single to the glory of God means a person's general orientation to life is centered around the Gospel of Jesus Christ. This orientation influences a person's conduct and attitude at all times. Generally, how conscientious you are in carrying out your various responsibilities in the Church indicates to what degree your motives are pure.

> But seek ye first the kingdom of God, and his righteousness; and all these things shall be added unto you. (Matthew 6:33.)

If your motives are pure, you will be entitled to inspiration in determining what desires you should seek.

> He that asketh in the Spirit asketh according to the will of God." (D&C 46:30.)

The Lord has admonished us to seek his support and inspiration in all our endeavors. (D&C 46:31; Moses 5:8.) You have the assurance that if you have an eye single to the glory of God you will be inspired to select righteous desires. (3 Nephi 19:24; D&C 50:29-30.)

It is your responsibility to be certain your desires are righteous. The Lord does not dictate what desires you should strive for.

President Kimball's Perception of Goals

Seeking specific rightous desires has an important place in our lives. President Spencer W. Kimball said concerning goals:

> We do believe in setting goals. We live by goals. In athletics we always have a goal. When we go to school, we have the goal of graduation and degrees. Our total existence is goal-oriented.
>
> We must have goals to make progress, encouraged by keeping records ... as the swimmer or the jumper or the runner does....

Progress is easier when it is timed, checked, and measured....

Goals are good. Laboring with a distant aim sets the mind in a higher key and puts us at our best.

Goals should always be made to a point that will make us reach and strain.[10]

It is most appropriate for [you]... to quietly, and with determination, set some serious personal goals in which [you]... will seek to improve by selecting certain things that [you]... will accomplish within a specified period of time. Even if [you]... are headed in the right direction, if [you]... are... without momentum [you]... will have too little influence.[11]

The first time you read this book answer the following question on a piece of paper.

Summarize President Kimball's feeling regarding goals.

If possible, discuss your answer with someone else who is reading this book.

Each time you reread this book:

Ask yourself: "Am I consistently setting goals?" If not, resolve to do so.

Guidelines for Setting Goals

Many of your goals (desires) grow out of expectations associated with your job, your schooling, your Church calling, etc. However, it is important that some of your goals (desires) are self imposed:

For behold, it is not meet that I should command in all things; for he that is compelled in all things, the same is a slothful and not a wise servant; wherefore he receiveth no reward.

Verily I say, men should be anxiously engaged in a good cause, and do many things of their own free will, and bring to pass much righteousness;

---

[10] Spencer W. Kimball, Regional Representatives Seminar, April 3, 1975.
[11] Spencer W. Kimball, "Boys Need Heroes Close By," *The Ensign*, May 1976, p. 46.

For the power is in them, wherein they are agents unto themselves. And inasmuch as men do good they shall in nowise lose their reward.

But he that doeth not anything until he is commanded, and receiveth a commandment with doubtful heart, and keepeth it with slothfulness, the same is damned. (D&C 58:26-29.)

As a general rule, it is much better to focus on a few pertinent goals at one time rather than attempting to focus on many goals simultaneously. You should use wisdom in determining how many goals you attempt to focus on at the same time according to your particular temperament, ability, etc.

Goals (desires), of course, need to be realistic, something you are not currently achieving, and something that will require a certain amount of mental exertion; otherwise you will not be required to use faith as a principle of power. You need to realize that the desire may not be easy to achieve, but you must maintain the faith that if you make a determined effort the Lord will prepare a way for your righteous goals to be accomplished. Your success in achieving the goal will be in direct proportion to your faith and efforts, *not your circumstances*. (read 1 Nephi 3:7.)

Throughout your life you should follow President Kimball's admonition to set goals for yourself. You should select goals in every facet of your life, not just goals related to your Church callings. You are entitled to draw on the powers of heaven in realizing any righteous desire, be it emotionally, socially, professionally, or academically oriented. Remember that the power of faith has "power, dominion, and authority over all things" and learn to approach everything you desire to achieve with the power of faith in mind. The Lord is willing and anxious to assist you in achieving your righteous desires if you will let him.

The Role of Faith in Achieving Goals

As you set goals for yourself, you should realize that goals fall into two basic categories. 1) Goals that can be accomplished as a result of the faith that prompts you to action.

These are goals where you can see clearly in your mind's eye how you can accomplish these goals through resolve and determination (e.g., that you will get up at 6 o'clock every morning, that you will refrain from being critical of others, that you will study the scriptures for a certain number of hours per week, etc.). 2) Goals that will require you to draw on the powers of heaven because you cannot see clearly in your mind's eye how they will be accomplished. These are goals that cannot be accomplished without the Lord's help; goals that require you to call down the powers of heaven to assist you in fulfilling them (e.g., that you will be instrumental in someone's conversion, that opportunities will be afforded you to earn $10,000 more per year).

When you set goals that cannot be attained or realized without the Lord's help, you should consistently remind yourself of the process of faith that is required to call down the powers of heaven. You will become frustrated if you set goals that require assistance from the powers of heaven to be realized and then fail to exercise the necessary faith that will allow your Father in Heaven the opportunity to assist you in attaining your particular goal. It is extremely important that you are conscious of the role of faith as a principle of power in the attainment of some goals. The faith that motivates you to have determination will make it possible to realize some goals, but faith as a principle of power is the key to achieving many other goals.

Learn to Commit

It is important to remember that a desire cannot be considered a goal until you are willing to commit yourself and resolve to do everything in your power to achieve the goal. You should not confuse things you merely consider achieving with those things you resolve to achieve.

Many of your goals will only involve a personal resolve on your part. In other instances, you will make commitments to others (e.g., ward leaders, teachers, etc.) and in some cases you must be willing to promise the Lord that you will do certain things in your effort to qualify yourself to draw on the powers of heaven (e.g., study the scriptures on a regular basis, go to the temple more often, fast more conscientiously, overcome a specific weakness). You should strive to develop an absolute faith in the Lord's promise, "I, the Lord, am bound when ye do what I say" (D&C 82:10).

Goals (Desires) Should Be Means, Not Ends

Concerning your goals in general, you should remember to consider them as means rather than ends. For instance, going on a mission is a goal for many members of the Church. Yet if missionaries are not willing to set specific goals after they are on a mission, they will not be very successful in their labors.

The same holds true for temple marriage; going through the temple is just the beginning of all that goes into a successful marriage. The same is true for goal setting in general. In no instance does the achievement of a goal mean you have arrived.

No matter how many goals you may achieve during a lifetime, you must look ahead to new goals. Unless you adopt the point of view that goals are means and not ends, you will experience a letdown every time you achieve a major goal. The achievement of goals should be an ongoing process—not the culmination of an effort that does not lead to a sustained effort to achieve additional goals. Consider the following example of goals as ends.

> The year after Bill and Mary Smith were married, Bill entered dental school. Their overriding goal was the completion of Bill's schooling. Bill and Mary started to have serious marital problems their second year in dental school. Yet they made up their minds to endure the situation with the anticipation that on the completion of his schooling that everything would change. After Bill graduated from dental school he and his wife discovered that they were still having serious marital problems, and their anticipation regarding the change in their life as a result of his being out of school did not materialize. Finally their relationship deteriorated to the point that they were divorced.

The above example shows how achievement of the goal to graduate from dental school had an adverse effect on the young couple because the goal was viewed as an end, not a means. This next example illustrates goals as a means.

> John and Sally Black were married during his senior year in college. Upon graduation he accepted a position with a company on the East coast. After a couple of years, John decided that it would be to his best interest professionally to go back to graduate school. After discussing the implications of this with his wife in terms of the sacrifices they would have to make as a result of reduced income, etc., she supported him in the decision.
>
> So the following year he started back to work on his advanced degree. Obviously they had to make some difficult adjustments in their standard of living in order to live at the income John had while he was completing his training. But he and his wife learned to resolve problems they encountered as they pursued the objective of completing his graduate degree. They soon found that during the last two years of his graduate training that they grew closer together as man and wife than they had in the three previous years of their marriage. In subsequent years he and his wife looked upon the time he was in graduate school as one of the most enjoyable times of their marriage.

In the process of achieving their goal, this young couple realized other benefits from their endeavors, because the goal was perceived as a means, and not an end in and of itself.

Seeking the Gifts of the Spirit

Your ability to achieve goals (righteous desires) generally, will be greatly enhanced if you first seek the gifts of the spirit. The gifts of the spirit are at your disposal to help you develop your full potential. The Lord expects you to earnestly seek specific gifts of the spirit through faith.

> Seek ye earnestly the best gifts. (D&C 46:8.)
>
> Behold, thou hast a gift, or thou shalt have a gift if thou wilt desire of me in faith, with an honest heart, believing in the power of Jesus Christ, or in my power which speaketh unto thee. (D&C 11:10.)
>
> And I would exort you, my beloved brethren, that ye remember that every good gift cometh of Christ.
>
> And I would exhort you, my beloved brethren, that ye remember

that he is the same yesterday, today, and forever, and that all these gifts of which I have spoken, which are spiritual, never will be done away, even as long as the world shall stand, only according to the unbelief of the children of men. (Moroni 10:18-19.)

Throughout your life consistently remind yourself that the gifts of the spirit are given "of God unto men, to profit them." (Moroni 10:8.)

The gifts of the spirit are at your disposal to assist you in all aspects of your life if you seek them. For example, there will be times in your life when you will be required to put in long hours in connection with your employment and/or your Church assignments. You are entitled to a gift of the spirit which will result in the literal renewal of your body. The Lord has promised that if you exercise faith and request it, you "shall not be weary in mind . . . neither in body, limb, nor joint." (D&C 84:80.)

Even though the Gift of the Holy Ghost is conferred on people when they are confirmed members of the Church, they still have the responsibility to prayerfully seek the gift. Receipt of the gift is not automatic. (3 Nephi 19:9-14; D&C 18:18.) In the course of our lives we need to seek the specific gifts associated with the Gifts of the Holy Ghost (e.g., the power of recall, a sure witness of the divinity of Christ, etc.).

Members of the Church who have callings as teachers should earnestly seek those gifts of the spirit that will make them effective. (Moroni 10:7-10.)

And the Spirit shall be given unto you by the *prayer of faith;* and if ye receive not the Spirit ye shall not teach. (D&C 42:14, italics added.)

Missionaries especially should seek the gift of the spirit that will give them the power to convince people that the gospel of Jesus Christ has been restored to the earth.

The Gift of Discernment

One gift every member of the Church of Jesus Christ should seek is the gift of discernment. As a member of the

Church you are given the basic gifts of discernment—the
Light of Christ and the Gift of the Holy Ghost. (Moroni
7:12-18; D&C 63:41.)

You are endowed with the ability to discern between good
and evil, whether or not a person is righteous (D&C 101:95;
Malachi 3:18; 3 Nephi 24:18.), and when the Spirit of God is
being manifest (D&C 46:23; I Corinthians 12:10.). If you are
desirous and earnestly seek it, if you strive to cultivate the
spirit of discernment, you will be endowed with even greater
powers of discernment. If you are successful in cultivating
this keener discernment, "the thoughts and intents of the
heart[s]" of people will be revealed to your mind. (D&C 33:1;
Hebrews 4:12.)

> Do you not know that you need the Spirit of the Almighty to look
> through a man and discern what is in his heart, while his face smiles
> upon you and his words flow as smoothly as oil.[12]
>
> The revelations of the Lord Jesus Christ, the spirit of truth will
> detect everything.... It will lead to God, the fountain of light, where
> the gate will be open, and the mind will be enlightened so that we shall
> see, know and understand things as they are.[13]
>
> I rejoice in the privilege of meeting with the Saints, in hearing
> them speak, and enjoying the influence that is within and around
> them. That influence opens to my understanding the true position of
> those who are endeavouring to serve their God. I do not require to hear
> them speak to enable me to know their feelings. Is it not also your
> experience that, when you meet persons in the street, in your houses, in
> your offices, or in the workshops, more or less of an influence attends
> them which conveys more than words can?... This knowledge is
> obtained through that invisible influence which attends intelligent
> beings, and betrays the atmosphere in which they delight to live.[14]

The power of discernment is evidenced many times in the
scriptures. (See Mosiah 13:6,7,11; Alma 7:17, 19, 20; 18:16, 18;
11:23-25, 12:3; Acts 5:1-10; 8:23; 3 Ne. 17:2,8; 28:6.)

---

[12]Brigham Young, *Journal of Discourses*, 3:225.
[13]Ibid. 13:336.
[14]Ibid. 8:57.

If in your association with other people you are able to discern their thoughts and feelings, your ability to know what to say and do will be greatly enhanced. Also, we are entitled to discern when people are evil and designing. The gift of discernment is at your disposal to assist you in all your responsibilities. However, it is your responsibility to prayerfully seek insight about and understanding of the gift of discernment. You must request the gift and tell the Lord why you want the gift, as well as explain what you will do with the gift if He bestows it upon you. Once you receive and cultivate the gift of discernment, your spiritual capabilities will be enhanced and you will be able to function with inspiration in all facets of your life.

The Greatest of All

The nature of the gifts of the spirit themselves appear to be virtually unlimited. Faith itself is a gift of the spirit. The nature of the gifts of the spirit seem to grow out of specific needs so it would not serve any purpose to try and list them. However, the gift of the spirit "which is the greatest of all" is charity. (Moroni 7:46.) We are admonished to seek this gift with all the energy of our hearts. (Moroni 7:48.) Moroni admonishes us to cleave (to adhere, cling) unto charity. (Moroni 7:46.) He also taught that if, in the final analysis, a man does not have charity, "he is nothing." (Moroni 7:46.) A person who cultivates the gift of charity will evidence certain characteristics. He will be long-suffering; he will be kind; he will not envy; he will not be puffed up; he will serve the interests of others; he will not be easily provoked; he will not think about evil things; he will rejoice in the truth; he will bear the infirmities, afflictions, etc. of this mortal life; he will believe all the truths associated with the gospel of Jesus Christ; he will evidence a prevailing hope in all the promises made in the holy scriptures; he will endure all things without waivering in his commitment to the Lord Jesus Christ.

> How many of you... are seeking for these gifts that God has promised to bestow? How many of you, when you bow before your

Heavenly Father in your family circle or in your secret places, contend
for these gifts to be bestowed upon you? How many of you ask the
Father, in the name of Jesus Christ, to manifest Himself to you
through these powers and these gifts? Or do you go along day by day
like a door turning on its hinges, without having any feeling upon the
subject, without exercising any faith whatever; content to be baptized
and be members of the Church, and to rest there, thinking that your
salvation is secure because you have done this?...

God is the same today as He was yesterday;... (He) is willing to
bestow these gifts upon His children. I know that God is willing to
heal the sick, that He is willing to bestow the gift of discerning of
spirits, the gift of wisdom, of knowledge and of prophecy, and other
gifts that may be needed.

If any of us are imperfect, it is our duty to pray for the gift that will
make us perfect. Have I imperfections? I am full of them. What is my
duty: To pray to God to give me the gifts that will correct these imperfections. If I am an angry man, it is my duty to pray for charity, which
suffereth long and is kind. Am I an envious man? It is my duty to seek
for charity, which envieth not. So with all the gifts of the Gospel. They
are intended for this purpose. No man ought to say, "Oh, I cannot help
this; it is my nature."He is not justified in it, for the reason that God
has promised to give strength to correct these things, and to give gifts
that will eradicate them.[15]

The gifts of the spirit will be yours: 1) if you acquire the
necessary insight about and an understanding of the gifts of
the spirit, 2) if you desire them, 3) if you ask the Lord to grant
you the gifts, and 4) if you comply with the laws that govern
the powers of heaven.

A man who has none of the gifts has no faith; and he deceives
himself, if he supposes he has.[16]

The first time you read this book answer the following
question on a piece of paper.

What should your attitude be regarding the gifts of the spirit,
including the gift of discernment?

[15]George Q. Cannon, *Millennial Star*, April 16, 1894, p. 260; as quoted in
Melchizedek Priesthood Personal Study Guide, 1977-78, pp. 153-154.
[16]Joseph Smith, *Teachings of the Prophet Joseph Smith* (S.L.C.: Deseret Book,
1976), p. 270.

If possible, discuss your answer with someone else who is reading this book.

Each time you reread this book:

Ask yourself the following questions:

What specific gifts and blessings of the spirit have you recently received or experienced?

Do you consistently seek the gifts of the spirit?

Have you sought after and received the gift of discernment?

II. Plead Your Case Before The Lord

Once you have made a decision about what you want the Lord to help you accomplish, your next step is to plead your case before the Lord. Go to the Lord in earnest prayer. Explain your rationale in selecting your particular desire, but most important, explain in great detail why you want the particular desire to be realized. Throughout history we see that the Lord is responsive to the request of mortal men if they go to him in faith and can present a strong case for the blessing they are seeking. In a very literal sense, you need to learn to reason with the Lord. A good example of this process is found in the eleventh chapter of Helaman:

> And it came to pass that when Nephi saw that the people had repented and did humble themselves in sackcloth, he cried again unto the Lord, saying:
>
> O Lord, behold this people repenteth; and they have swept away the band of Gadianton from amongst them insomuch that they have become extinct, and they have concealed their secret plans in the earth.
>
> Now, O Lord, because of this their humility wilt thou turn away thine anger, and let thine anger be appeased in the destruction of those wicked men whom thou hast already destroyed.
>
> O Lord, wilt thou turn away thine anger, yea, thy fierce anger, and cause that this famine may cease in this land.
>
> O Lord, wilt thou hearken unto me, and cause that it may be done according to my words, and send forth rain upon the face of the earth,

that she may bring forth her fruit, and her grain in the season of grain.

O Lord, thou didst hearken unto my words when I said, Let there be a famine, that the pestilence of the sword might cease; and I know that thou wilt, even at this time, hearken unto my words, for thou saidst that: If this people repent I will spare them.

Yea, O Lord, and thou seest that they have repented, because of the famine and the pestilence and destruction which has come unto them.

And now, O Lord, wilt thou turn away thine anger, and try again if they will serve thee? And if so, O Lord, thou canst bless them according to thy words which thou hast said. (Helaman 11:9-16.)

As you study the life of Joseph Smith, you will find that he never did receive new doctrine, etc. until he exerted himself and went to the Lord and requested clarification on a point. (Read the preface to Sections 76 and 132 of the Doctrine and Covenants.) Make every effort to exercise faith in the prophet Alma's promise:

Counsel with the Lord in all thy doings, and he will direct thee for good. (Alma 37:37.)

When you are seeking the powers of heaven to assist you in realizing a righteous desire, you should plead your case to your Heavenly Father daily until your desire is realized.

In your relationship with your Father in Heaven, you must ask in order to receive. Members of the Church have a tendency to be too general in their petitions to God (e.g., please bless, please help).You should resolve to be more specific in your request, expressing much more specifically the desires for which you are striving. Being more specific in prayers on a regular basis enhances the chance that your prayers will become earnest and sustained by faith. Unfortunately, most people do not petition the Lord unless they are faced with a crisis. You will find that your relationship with your Father in Heaven will be greatly enhanced if you are consistently seeking His help regarding your selected righteous desires instead of desires that grow out of a crisis in your life. Obviously, if you are seeking and experiencing the

Lord's help on a daily basis, when you are faced with a crisis your ability to exercise faith sufficient to call down the powers of heaven will be much greater. It is man's tendency to forget his dependence upon God when he is not faced with hardships.

> And because of this their great wickedness, and their boastings in their own strength, they were left in their own strength; therefore they did not prosper, but were afflicted and smitten, and driven before the Lamanites, until they had lost possession of almost all their lands. (Helaman 4:13)

> And thus we can behold how false, and also the unsteadiness of the hearts of the children of men; yea, we can see that the Lord in his great infinite goodness doth bless and prosper those who put their trust in him. (Helaman 12:1)

> They were slow to hearken unto the voice of the Lord their God; therefore, the Lord their God is slow to hearken unto their prayers, to answer them in the day of their trouble. In the day of their peace they esteemed lightly my counsel; but, in the day of their trouble, of necessity they feel after me. (D&C 101:7-8.)

The elect of God are those who do not lose sight of their dependence on God, even when they are not faced with adversity. You should make every effort to make your daily prayers earnest even when you are not faced with pressing problems. Your prayers will be mighty prayers if they are persuasive, because a mighty prayer is one that is heard and answered. If your prayers are not being answered, it may be due to your failure to pray with the power of faith or sufficiently plead your case before the Lord.

A critical factor in your effort to be effective when you plead your case before the Lord, is your ability to recognize your weaknesses. If you are successful in drawing close to the Lord, your perception of your weaknesses will be very clear. "If men come unto me I will show unto them their weakness" (Ether 12:27). If you have an abiding faith in the Lord's desire to bless and assist you, you will be motivated to strive to overcome your weaknesses. The Lord is responsive if He sees evidence that a person is going to be more resolved to keep the commandments, willing to be generous with his means in supporting the Kingdom of God, etc.

Our relationship with God is governed by laws. God is never capricious (inconsistent) in His disposition to bless us (see Mormon 9:9). He will always bless us according to our faith and worthiness (see D&C 130:20-21, 132:5).

If God's dealings with men were not totally consistent, He would cease to be God (see Mormon 9:19).

In your effort to solicit the Lord's help in realizing your righteous desires, you cannot rely on vocal prayers alone. You must learn to offer frequent silent prayers.

> And again, I command thee that thou shalt pray vocally as well as in thy heart.... (D&C 19:28.)

When you encounter a situation that causes you to doubt your ability to achieve your desire, request the Lord's help in maintaining an attitude of faith.

The first time you read this book answer the following question on a piece of paper.

> How should you go about pleading your case to your Father in Heaven?

If possible, discuss your answer with someone else who is reading this book.

III Exert Yourself Mentally

The thought process itself is the key to exercising faith. To a great extent we accomplish what we think about. In other words, what you think about today, tomorrow, or next month will mold your attitude and determine what you will accomplish during your life. Your life is influenced more by your own thoughts than anything else.

How could a person possibly become what he is *not* thinking? Nor is any thought, when persistently entertained, too small to have its effect. The "divinity that shapes our ends" is indeed in ourselves.[17]

In order to exercise faith, once you have prayerfully selected a righteous desire (e.g. increasing your earning power, activating an inactive child in your Sunday School class, etc.), you must become preoccupied with your desire. Faith can be gauged to a great extent by the amount of time spent thinking about your righteous desire. If your mind is not preoccupied with the thing you are trying to achieve, it is not a desire.

Do not confuse the preoccupation of worry and anxiety with the preoccupation involved in exercising faith. When your mind is prone to dwell on the adverse consequences of events which you assume you have very little control over, that is worry. In contrast, if your mind dwells on the possible consequences of various courses of action which you will control to a great extent, you are exercising faith.

The mind is like a field: you will harvest whatever you plant in it if it is nourished. You should learn to follow the Lord's admonition:

> Look unto me in every thought; doubt not, fear not. (D&C 6:36.)

Research has demonstrated that most people use their minds in constructive thinking only about ten percent of the time. Similarly, the amount of faith they exercise is extremely limited.

We are commanded not to doubt:

> Doubt not, but be believing.... (Mormon 9:27.)

> ... where doubt and uncertainty are there faith is not, nor can it be. For doubt and faith do not exist in the same person at the same time; so that persons whose minds are under doubts and fears cannot have unshaken confidence; and where unshaken confidence is not there faith is weak.[18]

---

[17] Spencer W. Kimball, *The Miracle of Forgiveness*, op. cit., pp. 104-105, italics in original.

[18] Joseph Smith, *Lectures on Faith*, op. cit., pp. 59-60.

Thinking negatively does not require any effort; maintaining a believing frame of mind, however, requires an exerted effort over a sustained period of time.

By the process of faith, thoughts produce an effect as literal as physical exertion. Your thoughts, more than anything else, will be the determining factor in what you accomplish during your life.

Control Your Mind

Exercising faith in the powers of heaven is a fairly simple process but it involves continual mental exertion.

> When a man works by faith he works by mental exertion instead of by physical force.[19]

Mental exertion involves the following basic steps: (1) train yourself to be conscious of your thoughts, (2) learn to scrutinize your thoughts to determine if they add to or detract from your faith, and (3) if a thought detracts from your faith, replace it with a thought that is based on faith, such as reminding yourself of the Lord's goodness, thinking of his willingness to bless you, or recalling his numerous promises in the scriptures that if we ask in faith he will bless us. If you learn to put forth the necessary mental exertion, you will be successful in cultivating the faith required to qualify for the power and force for righteousness that comes through faith.

In order to exert yourself mentally you must have power and dominion over your mind. You cannot allow your mind to be easily distracted or to focus on something that is extraneous to the purpose or object of your desired blessing. For instance, when you call upon the Lord for his blessings, do you find yourself thinking about things you need to do, or do other mundane preoccupations pop into your mind? The next time you pray or meditate, see if you have power and control over your mind sufficient to keep it from wandering during your attempt to communicate with the Lord. Consider

---

[19] Joseph Smith, *Lectures on Faith*, op. cit., p. 61, italics added.

how offensive it would be if a person to whom you were speaking were reading a book. In the same way, our behavior is offensive to the Lord when we are speaking with him and allow our minds to be distracted. Until you learn to discipline your mind and have complete control over it, you will be expressly limited in your capacity to exercise faith. The full power of the mind is only realized when it is specifically focused and directed to a specific end.

> ... if therefore thine eye [mind's eye] be single, thy whole body shall be full of light. (Matthew 6:22.)

If you allow your mind to dwell randomly on incidental or mundane preoccupations, you will be limited in your ability to draw on the power of faith and your mind will not be a source of power for you.

You will discover, however, that as you attempt to control and focus your mind, the devil will bring things to your view to distract you. When you can control your mind and not allow it to be distracted, you will be able to exercise unlimited faith and unlock the powers of heaven by your faith.

> The greatest mystery a man ever learned, is to know how to control the human mind, and bring every faculty and power of the same in subjection to Jesus Christ; this is the greatest mystery we have to learn while in these tabernacles of clay.[20]

You need to consistently remind yourself that your mind is literally the key to unlocking the powers of heaven. You must learn to control your mind.

> It [the mind] is the agent of the Almighty clothed with mortal tabernacles, and we must learn to discipline it, and bring it to bear on one point, and not allow the Devil to interfere and confuse it, nor divert it from the great object we have in view....
>
> If we could control our own minds, we could control our children and our families and the kingdom of God, and see that everything went right, and with much more ease than we do now.[21]

---

[20] Brigham Young, *Journal of Discourses*, 1:46–47.
[21] Orson Hyde, *Journal of Discourses*, 7:153.

You need to be able to control your mind so it is not distracted by events or other preoccupations around you and make it focus with all its force on a particular problem you are trying to solve or blessing you are seeking.

> If a person trains his mind to walk in the spirit, and brings his whole mind to bear upon its operations, and upon the principles of faith which are calculated to put him in possession of the power of God, how much greater will be his facilities for obtaining knowledge....[22]

In our present society music has often become "opium" for the mind. Listening to good music is fine, but when a person turns to music as an escape hours on end, it becomes detrimental. If a person spends hours observing sporting events but does not engage in any physical exercise, his body will suffer. As it is with the body, so it is with the mind. If we allow our mind to engage in things which do not require any effort such as listening to popular music, our mind and spirit will suffer.

The Eye of Faith

One of the best ways to exert yourself mentally is to create a mental picture of the thing for which you are striving and to repeatedly bring this picture to mind. In a very literal sense, desired ends must be created spiritually in the mind before they can be realized. Through the process of faith you can see clearly in your mind what you can accomplish with the Lord's help. Being allowed to see clearly what we can accomplish with the Lord's help is a form of a vision. Seeing things in your mind's eye is seeing with the "eye of faith." (Alma 5:15, Ether 12:19.)

You can exert yourself mentally by asking yourself questions and then carefully weighing various answers or by exploring various solutions to a problem and carefully weighing the projected consequence of each alternative. You

---

[22] Orson Pratt, *Journal of Discourses*, 7:155-156.

can also exert yourself mentally by rehearsing things in your mind. The mind is capable of rehearsing anything you are trying to accomplish such as taking a test, running a race, giving a speech, or writing a paper. This whole process can be facilitated if you will learn to devote certain periods of time each day to meditation.

Ponder it in Your Hearts

The dictionary says that *ponder* means "to weigh in the mind; to deliberate about; to review mentally; to meditate." Moroni thus used the term as he closed his record:

> Behold, I would exhort you that when ye shall read these things . . . that ye would . . . *ponder* it in your hearts. (Moroni 10:3 italics added.)

"Pondering is, in my feeling," said President Romney, "a form of prayer."[23] Such periods of meditation should be devoted exclusively to prayer (during which you reason with the Lord) or to mental exertion regarding your righteous desires.

Obviously, when you are praying you are in a position to focus your mind exclusively on your dealings and relationship with the Lord. However, to exercise greater faith you need to learn to focus your mind on your righteous desires during those numerous minutes when you are not required to deal mentally with anything in particular. This can be while you prepare to leave in the morning, while you are eating or driving, or after you retire for the night. Most people have formed very poor mental habits. They make no effort to control or direct their thinking during these segments of the day.

People who do not make an exerted effort to control their thoughts are prone to dwell on petty feelings (e.g., resentments, offenses, jealousies, anxieties, strife, contempt, self-pity) or let their mind aimlessly wander.

---

[23] Marion G. Romney, "Magnifying One's Calling in the Priesthood," *The Ensign*, July 1973, pp. 90-91.

Significant insights and discovories are made by people who have learned to discipline their minds to the extent that they can concentrate on one problem for long periods of time. This is very evident in the lives of the prophets, Church leaders, and great inventors, such as Sir Isaac Newton and Albert Einstein. Newton, for example, concentrated the energies of his mind for many years on the subject of mathematical and mechanical problems which ultimately led to the discovery of the new form of geometry. By bringing all of the energies of his intellect to bear upon a given subject or problem, he gained control of his mind and was able to make many other important discoveries. The same holds true for anyone else. The following account was reported by Elder Boyd K. Packer.

> I have a friend who bought a business. A short time later he suffered catastrophic reverses and there just didn't seem to be any way out for him. Finally it got so bad that he couldn't sleep, so for a period of time he followed the practice of getting up about three o'clock in the morning and going to the office. There, with a paper and a pen, he would ponder and pray and write down every idea that came to him as a possible solution or contributions to the solution of his problem.

> It wasn't long before he had several possible directions in which he could go, and it wasn't much longer than that until he had chosen the best of them. But he had earned an extra bonus. His notes showed, after he went over them, that he had discovered many hidden resources he had never noticed before. He came away more independent and successful than he would ever have been if he hadn't suffered those reverses.

> There is a lesson in this experience. A year or two later he was called to preside over a mission overseas. His business was so independent and so well set up that when he came back he didn't return to it. He now has someone else managing it, and has been able to give virtually all his time to the blessing of others.[24]

Serve God with Your Mind

As you concentrate on achieving your goals (desires), continually remind yourself that if you exercise the necessary faith, the Lord will assist you in achieving them. Learning to

---

[24]Boyd K. Packer, *Teach Ye Diligently* (S.L.C.: Deseret Book, 1975), pp. 204-205.

think positively about something over a long period of time may be difficult because we must formulate new habits, and new habits are not easily formed. If you dwell on supposed obstacles to achieving your goal (desire), your desire to realize your goals will not be sufficiently strong to motivate persistence.

When you focus your thoughts on the achievement of righteous desires, you are serving the Lord with your heart, might, and mind. (See D&C 4:2.) Often, in our efforts to serve the Lord with our strength (time and energy), we fall short because we fail to serve the Lord with our heart (emotions and sentiments), might (will power), and mind (intellect and reasoning ability). You will find your effectiveness in achieving your righteous desires will be greatly enhanced when you learn to control your mind and focus your mental energies.

If you are consistently looking to the Lord to assist you in achieving various righteous desires, you will be complying with the Lord's admonition to "let thy thoughts be directed unto the Lord." (Alma 37:36.)

What you think about is either conducive to faith or distracts from your ability to exercise faith. Your thoughts with respect to faith cannot be neutral. If your thoughts are not productive or edifying, you have the responsibility of replacing them with productive or edifying thoughts. The Lord has warned "if ye do not watch yourselves, and your thoughts, . . . ye must perish." (Mosiah 4:30.) It will enhance your initiative to control your thoughts if you consistently remind yourself of the commandment to refrain from idleness. (Alma 38:12; D&C 42:42; 60:13; 75:3, 29; 88:124.) This also applies to idle thoughts as the Lord has commanded us to "cast away" our idle thoughts. (D&C 88:69.)

The power of faith through thought can be latent or apparent, concentrated or diluted, used or unused. Your ability to draw on this power will increase with effort; the more you exert yourself in controlling your thoughts, the more your capacity to focus your mind will increase.

The first time you read this book answer the following question on a piece of paper.

How do you exert yourself mentally?

If possible, discuss your answer with someone else who is reading this book.

Each time you reread this book:

Ask yourself the following question:

To what degree do your thoughts focus on the attainment of righteous desires and to what degree do you allow mundane preoccupations, doubts, and fears to occupy your mind?

Alter Your Thoughts

Some people are prone to blame their circumstances for their failure to realize their righteous desires. As you understand the process of faith, you will realize that you can change your circumstances by changing your attitude and exercising faith.

A man is literally what he thinks, his character being the complete sum of all his thoughts.[25]

The thought in your mind at this moment is contributing, however infinitesimally, almost imperceptibly to the shaping of your soul,... even passing and idle thoughts leave their impression.[26]

I will know what you are if you tell me what you think about when you don't have to think.[27]

For as he thinketh in his heart, so is he. (Proverbs 23:7.)

If you radically alter your thoughts, you will be astonished at how rapidly the material conditions of your life will be transformed. Your thoughts dictate your circumstances because thoughts govern habits and habits dictate circum-

[25] Spencer W. Kimball, The Miracle of Forgiveness, op. cit., p. 103.
[26] David O. McKay, quoted in The Miracle of Forgiveness, op. cit., p. 105.
[27] David O. McKay, True to the Faith, (S.L.C.: Bookcraft, 1966), p. 270.

stances. All actions, both spontaneous (unpremeditated) and premeditated are the product of our thoughts.

You exercise your agency in what you think about as literally as you do in your actions. Of all the creatures on earth, man alone can change his thought pattern and become the architect of his destiny. Unfortunately, many members of the Church make very little effort to discipline their thoughts. They make some effort to avoid vulgar and obscene thoughts, but they do not make an exerted effort to control and direct their thoughts. When a person is groping in life, we say "he has not found himself." This statement is not accurate. Self is created, not found.

> Each one of us is the architect of his own fate; and he is unfortunate indeed who will try to build himself without the inspiration of God, without realizing that he grows from within, not from without.[28]

At the final judgment, our thoughts and the intents of our hearts are going to be revealed. (D&C 88:109.) President Kimball has stated that since the thoughts and intents of our hearts are going to be revealed, it follows that they are being recorded.

> Men's deeds and thoughts must be recorded in heaven,... it is not too great a stretch of the imagination in modern days to believe that our thoughts as well will be recorded by some means now known only to higher beings![29]

The Lord has said all of us will be judged by our thoughts:

> ...our thoughts will also condemn us;... (Alma 12:14.)

It is sobering to realize our every thought is being recorded and will be a critical factor in our final judgement.

Some people fail to realize the influence of their thoughts on their lives, and consequently they make very little effort to

---

[28] David O. McKay, "True End of Life," *The Instructor*, January 1964, p. 1.
[29] Spencer W. Kimball, *The Miracle of Forgiveness*, op. cit., pp. 109 & 111.

discipline their thoughts. A person's life will lack direction and meaning unless he is able to define very clearly in his mind what he wants to accomplish in life and then train his mind to focus on his righteous desires.

The first time you read this book answer the following question on a piece of paper.

How can you change your circumstances?

If possible, discuss your answer with someone else who is reading this book.

Each time you reread this book:

If you find yourself being controlled by your circumstances, resolve to exercise the necessary faith to change your circumstances.

IV. Sustained Effort

You will begin to feel the power of faith in your life when you have been successful in maintaining the necessary mental discipline coupled with righteous living *for several consecutive weeks.* You must resolve to make an exerted effort to exercise faith in your ability to draw on the powers of heaven over a sustained period of time; you will never experience the power of faith to any great extent unless you are willing to maintain your efforts over time. Resolve to test this principle by putting forth the necessary effort even though it may be difficult at first.

For example, if your righteous desire is to cultivate the gift of discernment, test the process by faithfully following the steps prescribed in this book for several consecutive weeks in your effort to cultivate the gift.

As you are successful in using faith as a principle of power in your ability to achieve a righteous desire, repeat the process for another righteous desire, then another, and then another. Once you are truly converted to faith as a principle of power, you will come to the realization that there is virtually no limit to what you can accomplish if you are able to call down the powers of heaven to assist you.

If you will consistently work at using faith as a principle of power, you will find the process becomes easier until finally it becomes almost spontaneous. Your ultimate desire should be to control your mind so that you think about only the things that you want to think about. To achieve this you must become conscious of your thoughts, learn to scrutinize them, and finally, replace doubts and fears with thoughts that are conducive to faith. As you learn to control and direct your thinking you will be able to draw upon the powers of heaven to assist you in all aspects of life.

The first time you read this book answer the following questions on a piece of paper.

Generally, how long must you focus on a righteous desire before you begin to experience faith as a principle of power?

How does a person become converted to faith as a principle of power?

In what facets of your life should you employ faith as a principle of power?

If possible, discuss your answers with someone else who is reading this book.

Each time you reread this book:

Ask yourself the following questions:

Are you truly converted to the principle of faith?

Are you able to draw on the powers of heaven to assist you in every facet of your life?

Chapter Four

Faith Will Be Tried

Even though the Lord will assist you in achieving righteous goals, you need to be aware that your faith will be tried. Generally, your faith will be tried under two sets of conditions: When you first begin to look to your Father in Heaven earnestly for help in realizing specific ends and when you are seeking desires that require major intervention from the powers of heaven.

From the very beginning the pattern followed by the Lord in granting blessings has been: 1) the Lord allows the person seeking the blessing to be tested and tried and 2) once the person humbles himself and proves his faith by perseverance and sustained faithfulness, the righteous desires are granted.

It was not until Father Adam had demonstrated his determination to be faithful to the commandments of the Lord that he received a rich outpouring of the spirit (see Moses 5:4-12). We see this same pattern illustrated in the lives of other prophets of the Old Testament such as Abraham, Jacob and Moses. It is interesting to note that the Savior himself was not exempt from this pattern. (Read Matthew 4:11; Mosiah 3:7; Alma 7:11-12.)

A period of proving, or a trial of faith, is necessary to see if someone who is seeking a special blessing from the Lord will remain faithful in the face of opposition. If a person understands that his faith is going to be tried, it gives him a greater resolve to be persistent in times of opposition. Your trial of faith basically serves four functions: 1) It determines if a goal you are seeking is truly a desire; 2) it lets you learn if you are really dedicated to the Lord; 3) it is a means of purging you so that you become clean, pure, and spotless—literally free from the blood and sins of the world; and 4) it humbles you and brings you to the realization that you cannot rely on the "arm of flesh." (see 2 Ne. 4:34; 28:31; Helaman 4:13; D&C 1:19.) As you learn to endure your trials of faith you will literally become a new creature in Christ and your body will be cleansed of all sin and renewed by the Spirit of the Lord. (Alma 5:14-15, 19; D&C 84:33.) This is the process of rebirth and sanctification.

It is extremely important that you realize that trials of faith are a necessary part of the sanctification process by which we are purified by the Spirit of God.

> And he shall purify the sons of Levi, and purge [his people] as gold and silver, that they may offer unto the Lord an offering in righteousness. (3 Ne. 24:3; D&C 128:24.)

> Therefore, they must needs be chastened and tried, even as Abraham, who was commanded to offer up his only son. For all those who will not endure chastening, but deny me, cannot be sanctified. (D&C 101:4-5; 136:31.)

> Nevertheless they did fast and pray oft, and did wax stronger and stronger in their humility, and firmer and firmer in the faith of Christ, unto the filling their souls with joy and consolation, yea, even to the purifying and the sanctification of their hearts, which sanctification cometh because of their yielding their hearts unto God. (Helaman 3:35.)

Opposition plays a very important part in this process, for by overcoming opposition and enduring affliction we are, in a very literal sense, purged and made clean. When you endure opposition by serving the Lord to the utmost of your ability—

no matter how limited your ability is—the grace of God is sufficient to intervene in your behalf; you have the promise that you can become "perfect in Christ." (Read Moroni 10:32-33.) It is by this means that you can qualify for the Spirit of the Lord in spite of the limitations of the flesh.

The first time you read this book answer the following question on a piece of paper.

Why does the Lord allow our faith to be tried?

If possible, discuss your answer with someone else who is reading this book.

Your Own Trial of Faith

The nature of a person's trial of faith will be based on his particular temperament and disposition; the thing that would test one person's faith would not necessarily test another's.

> God will feel after you, and he will take hold of you and wrench your very heart strings, and if you cannot stand it you will not be fit for an inheritance in the Celestial Kingdom of God."[30]

Your trial of faith will bring you to the realization that you cannot succeed by relying on the "arm of flesh." By yourself you are extremely limited in being able to accomplish your righteous desires. However, when you humble yourself, fully realizing that you cannot succeed without the Lord's help, and submit yourself to your Father in Heaven and become earnest in your desires, he will extend himself to you. Every man can endure his trial of faith whatever it may be, by remaining faithful and obedient in spite of opposition, inconvenience, discomfort, or pain.

The Lord expects you to "be patient in affliction", not complaining about your problems or discomforts. (D&C

---

[30] Joseph Smith, quoted by President Harold B. Lee in *The Ensign*, January, 1973, p. 62, italics added.

31:9.) For example, when you talk to others, accentuate the positive aspects of your life circumstances. The ability to endure hardships patiently is a great virtue and will bring you maturity, stability and spiritual strength.

> And the Lord said unto them also: Go forth among the Lamanites, thy brethren, and establish my word; yet *ye shall be patient in long-suffering and afflictions*, that ye may show forth good examples unto them in me,... (Alma 17:11, italics added.)

> And if thou shouldst be cast into the pit, or into the hands of murderers, and the sentence of death passed upon thee; if thou be cast into the deep; if the billowing surge conspire against thee; if fierce winds become thine enemy; if the heavens gather blackness, and all the elements combine to hedge up the way; and above all, if the very jaws of hell shall gape open the mouth wide after thee, know thou, my son, that *all these things shall give thee experience, and shall be for thy good*. The Son of Man hath descended below them all. Art thou greater than he? (D&C 122:7-8, italics added.)

> ...but we glory in tribulations also: knowing that tribulation worketh patience; And patience, experience; and experience, hope. (Romans 5:3-4.)

> ...for behold they were naked, and their skins were worn exceedingly because of being bound with strong cords. And they also had suffered hunger, thirst, and all kinds of afflictions; nevertheless they were patient in all their sufferings. (Alma 20:29)

> For verily I say unto you, blessed is he that keepeth my commandments, whether in life or in death; and *he that is faithful in tribulation, the reward of the same is greater in the kingdom of heaven. Ye cannot behold with your natural eyes, for the present time, the design of your God concerning those things which shall come hereafter, and the glory which shall follow after much tribulation. For after much tribulation come the blessings*. Wherefore the day cometh that ye shall be crowned with much glory; the hour is not yet, but is nigh at hand. (D&C 58:2-4, italics added.)

If you stay close to the Spirit, you will not be overwhelmed by the trials of your faith. You have the assurance that with the Spirit as your companion you can resolve difficulties.

Spirituality impels one to conquer difficulties and acquire more and more strength.[31]

The first time you read this book answer the following questions on a piece of paper.

How will your faith be tried?

Have you responded faithfully when you were confronted with trials and tribulation?

If possible, discuss your answers with someone else who is reading this book.

Men Who Endured Their Trials of Faith

One of the greatest examples of a trial of faith is recorded in the Book of Alma and involves the missionary labors of the sons of Mosiah. These men were responsible for the conversion of a large segment of the Lamanite population, even though the Lamanites were described as "a wild and a hardened and a ferocious people," (Alma 17:14.) and appeared as though they were not receptive to the gospel message. The key to the mass conversion of the Lamanites was the Spirit of the Lord that accompanied the sons of Mosiah in their labors. Even in the limited account that we have of their missionary labors it is evident that they experienced a trial of their faith.

... for they had many afflictions; they did suffer much, both in body and in mind, such as hunger, thirst and fatigue, and also much labor in the spirit.

... and they fasted much and prayed much that the Lord would grant unto them a portion of his Spirit to go with them, and abide with them, that they might be an instrument in the hands of God to bring, if it were possible, their brethren, the Lamanites, to the knowledge of the truth, ...

And the Lord said unto them also: Go forth among the Lamanites, thy brethren, and establish my word; yet ye shall be patient in long-suffering and afflictions, that ye may show forth good examples unto

---

[31] David O. McKay, "True End of Life," The Instructor, January, 1964, p. 2.

them in me, and I will make an instrument of thee in my hands unto the salvation of many souls. (Alma 17:5,9,11.)

The following quotation gives an excellent synopsis of this entire experience.

And this is the account of Ammon and his brethren, their journeyings in the land of Nephi, their sufferings in the land, their sorrows, and their afflictions, and their incomprehensible joy, . . . (Alma 28:8.)

In other words, even though they suffered much, they ultimately experienced great joy and satisfaction in their labors because they endured their trials of faith.

Wilford Woodruff's Experience

One of the most successful missionaries in the history of the restored Church was Wilford Woodruff. You can probably recall hearing repeated references to the success Wilford Woodruff experienced during his missionary labors. Most people fail to realize, however, that he also experienced great hardships throughout his mission and that his faith was sorely tried before he started to have success. The following excerpts from his own journal will give you some idea of the trial of faith to which Wilford Woodruff was subjected.

We cared not to go to houses and get food, so we picked and ate raw corn, and slept on the ground—We had walked all day without anything to eat, and were very hungry and tired. Neither the minister nor his wife would give us anything to eat, nor let us stay overnight, because we were Mormons; and the only chance we had was to go twelve miles farther down the river, to an Osage Indian trading post kept by a Frenchman named Jereu; and the wicked priest who would not give us a piece of bread lied to us about the road, and sent us across the swamp, and we wallowed knee-deep in mud and water till ten o'clock at night in trying to follow the crooked river. We then left the swamp, and put out into the prairie, to lie in the grass for the night.[32]

These are but brief excerpts from Wilford Woodruff's journal, but they indicate the tremendous ordeal he encountered during the early months of one of his missions. Five months elapsed before he and his companion had a baptism.

---

[32] Matthias F. Cowley, *Wilford Woodruff*, (SLC: Bookcraft, 1964), pp. 47–48.

A very interesting sidelight is that his companion finally became discouraged and returned home leaving Wilford Woodruff alone for a period in the mission field. Shortly after this, Wilford Woodruff started to meet with a great deal of success.

Today, President Kimball is a classic example of someone who has endured various trials of faith. In the course of his life he has endured many trials of faith (Bell's palsy, chronic tonsilitis, evil spirits, excessive boils, heart attacks, cancer of the throat, open heart surgery).

Maintaining Faith in the Face of Opposition

Fortunately, there are several things you can do when your faith is being tried:

1. Reflect on this statement by President Kimball:

> I have on occasion cited the need for many reservoirs in our lives to provide for our needs. I have said, "Some reservoirs are to store water. Some are to store food, as we do in our family welfare program and as Joseph did in the land of Egypt during the seven years of plenty. There should also be reservoirs of knowledge to meet the future needs; reservoirs of courage to overcome the floods of fear that put uncertainty in our lives; reservoirs of physical strength to help us meet the frequent burdens of work and illness; reservoirs of goodness; reservoirs of stamina; reservoirs of faith.
>
> Yes, especially reservoirs of faith, so that when the world presses in upon us, we stand firm and strong; when the temptations of a decaying [and, I should add, increasingly permissive and wicked] world about us draw on our energies, sap our spiritual vitality, and seek to pull us down, we need a storage of faith that can carry youth, and later adults, over the dull, the difficult, the terrifying moments; disappointments; disillusionments; and years of adversity, want, confusion, and frustration.[33]

2. Read and reflect upon the following scriptures:

> I do know that whosoever shall put their trust in God shall be supported in their trials, and their troubles, and their afflictions,... (Alma 36:3.)

---

[33] Spencer W. Kimball, "The Foundations of Righteousness," *The Ensign*, November 1977, p. 5.

Come unto me, all ye that labor and are heavy laden, and I will give you rest. Take my yoke upon you, and learn of me; for I am meek and lowly in heart: and ye shall find rest unto your souls. For my yoke is easy, and my burden is light. (Matthew 11:28-30.)

3. When you feel a need for a spiritual lift in times of disappointment or discouragment, read and reread Alma 17-26. If you will read these chapters prayerfully you will be inspired and given the strength to endure your trials of faith.

4. Memorize the phrase "For after much tribulation come the blessings." (D&C 58:4.)

5. Identify a personal collection of favorite scriptures and quotations and read them when your faith is being tried. Suggestions: Alma 26:23-35; 2 Corinthians 1:4-7.

6. Reread this book.

7. Read the following scriptures: D&C 98:3; 68:6; 24:8; 31:9; 101:4-5; 88:63; 122:7-8; 58:2-4; Moses 5:4-12; Alma 26:27; 31:30-31, 38; 7:11-12; 36:3; 17:14; 17:5, 9, 11; 28:8; 20:29; Mosiah 3:7; 23:21; Matthew 1:11; 11:28-30; Hebrews 5:8; Acts 5:38-42; Romans 8:35-39; 5:3-4; 2 Corinthians 6:4-6; John 16:33; Moroni 10:32-33.

Caution

No matter who you are and even if you are consistently prayerful in the process of selecting righteous desires, there will be times when you will begin to exercise faith in a desire that is not approved by your Father in Heaven. When this is the case you will experience a stupor of thought and will find it virtually impossible to focus your mind on your desires. When this happens you should cease your effort to exercise faith regarding the desire and make every effort to prayerfully determine why the desire is not appropriate.

In your effort to exercise faith, it is your responsibility to insure that you do not confuse either your lack of personal worthiness, desire, personal discipline, or a trial of faith with the stupor of thought just described. If you are sensitive to the spirit, you will be able to discern very clearly between a trial of faith and the stupor of thought that occurs when a desire, for one reason or another, is inappropriate.

With this understanding you should be able to consistently have the assurance that your desires are righteous. You should keep this caution in mind because through persistence, it is possible to realize desires that in the wisdom of the Lord are not in your best interest. The Lord honors our agency in the desires we seek.

Summary

The following is a summary of the understanding, insights, procedures, etc. required to call down the powers of heaven to bless your life.

1. A clear understanding of faith as a principle of power.

2. A realization that the powers of heaven are governed by our individual faith.

3. Live righteously.

4. Prayerfully select righteous goals (desires).

5. Specify your goals (desires) in writing.

6. Specify when your goals (desires) will be attained.

7. Plead your case before the Lord, telling Him what effort or sacrifice you are willing to make to achieve the goal (desire).

8. Consistently think about your goal (desire).

9. Use all of your willpower to think positively about your potential to achieve your goal (desire) with the Lord's help.

10. Consistently remind yourself that the added power and strength from God that is at your disposal is based on your individual faith.

11. Remember the Lord is anxious to grant your righteous desires if you will but qualify yourself.

12. Make your specific goal (desire) a matter of constant prayer.

13. Pray that the Lord will enhance your ability to exercise faith as a principle of power.

14. When you face a situation that causes you to doubt your ability to achieve your goal (desire), learn to offer a mental prayer to request the Lord's help, then exercise faith that he will help you, remembering that if you lack faith you deny the Lord the opportunity to assist you.

15. Repeatedly reflect on the promise made by the Savior: "Ask, and it shall be given you; seek, and ye shall find; knock, and it shall be opened unto you." (Mat. 7:7.)

16. Recognize at the outset that your faith most likely will be tried.

17. Make certain you do your part in your effort to achieve righteous goals (desires).

Chapter Five

Guidelines
To Enhance Your Faith

Specify A Plan of Action

Once you have prayerfully selected a righteous desire, in many instances you will find it helpful to reduce your plan of action to writing. Generally, your plan will include the following:

Your Desire

State your desire (goal) as specifically as possible. It should include the time period in which you intend to achieve your desire (e.g., meet a family this week who will be baptized by the end of the month).

Your Resolves

Everything you will do to accomplish the particular goal. These are things that are in your power to do in order that your righteous desires will be accomplished (e.g., I will tract at least three hours per day, I will keep all the mission rules, I will practice various door approaches every morning with my companion, etc.).

The Help You Will Need from the Lord

The specific blessings that you desire to receive which will require your drawing upon the powers of heaven (e.g., touch the hearts of a family and prepare them for the message of the restoration, guide us to the home of the family, etc.).

Your Commitment

A list of the things you are willing to do in order to qualify for the Lord's help. Your commitments should be established under inspiration and should be commitments which will demonstrate your worthiness and dedication and the strength of your desire in receiving assistance from the Lord (e.g., I will not harbor any negative feelings toward my companion, but will express love for him each day; I will read the scriptures each day, etc.).

Example:

Brother Johnson was just called to be the Deacons Advisor. He prayerfully selected the goal to teach his Priesthood lessons in such a way that each member of the class would be touched by the Spirit and receive knowledge and insights that would help them in their personal lives. The following was his plan of action:

My Desire:

1. To teach my Priesthood lessons each week in such a way that each member of the class will be touched by the Spirit and receive knowledge and insights that will help them in their personal lives.

My Resolves:

1. Study each lesson for two hours each Sunday and for thirty minutes each day of the week.
2. Meditate for 15 minutes each day regarding the members of the class and their needs.
3. Study the scriptures for thirty minutes a day.
4. Get to know each member of the class personally.
5. Solicit feedback from individual class members.

Help I Will Need from the Lord:

1. Reveal to my mind the needs and dispositions of those I teach.

2. Be inspired in how to present each lesson so it will be interesting and meet the specific needs of my students.

3. Help the class members understand the truths I present.

4. Have the Spirit of the Holy Ghost manifest itself during each lesson.

5. Calm my nerves.

My Commitments

1. Fast about my desire at least once a month.

2. Express my love and appreciation to others *much* more.

It is important that you be guided by the Lord in establishing your plan of action. As you prayerfully approach Him, He will bring to your mind an understanding of things you need to do in order to accomplish your desire (e.g., Brother Johnson took the above plan of action to the Lord and asked for further guidance. The thought came to his mind that he was being overly critical of one of his business associates. He then added a third commitment not to find fault with his associate.)

As the Lord guides you in formulating a plan of action that will result in the realization of your righteous desires, you will develop an abiding faith that divine blessings always follow obedience to the laws upon which these blessings are predicated (see D&C 130:20).

The first time you read this book answer the following question on a piece of paper.

How can specifying your plan of action in writing assist you in your effort to exercise faith as a principle of power?

If possible, discuss your answer with someone else who is reading this book.

Measure Your Faith

Very basic to the process of goal setting is consistent and accurate accounting of your performance in achieving your goals. Three basic steps are necessary in the process to make an accurate accounting of your performance with respect to your goals: (1) reduce your goals to writing, (2) measure your performance against your predetermined goals on a regular basis, and (3) revise your goals under inspiration.

Step 1: *Reduce Your Goals to Writing*—Goals should always be reduced to writing in terms of what you intend to accomplish or do. In addition, you should specify when you intend to accomplish a specific goal unless it is an ongoing goal, such as reading the scriptures for half an hour each day. Where you record your goals is a matter of personal preference. Some people find it advantageous to record their goals on 3 x 5 cards which they carry with them in their shirt pockets. Others record their goals and post them in conspicuous places. You should formulate a method of recording your goals that is appropriate for you.

> We must have goals to make progress, encouraged by keeping records.[34]

Step 2: *Measure Your Performance Against Your Predetermined Goals on a Regular Basis*—The value of goals will be lost unless you follow President Kimball's advice to measure and check your performance against predetermined goals on a regular basis. You should review your progress daily.

Example:

> Every morning Elder Bennett writes down what he intends to accomplish that day. Each night just before bed he evaluates his performance for that day. On Sundays he looks at the week's goals and plans for the next week. This Sunday he wrote to his district leader that he felt good about all of his goals except one. Earlier in his mission he had set a goal to read 20 pages a day from the Book of Mormon. By the end of his first month in the mission field it became apparent that with the time required to memorize the discussions, this goal was unrealistic. He informed his district leader that he had modified this goal to 10 pages a day, three days a week.

You account in several ways. For example, in your personal prayers you should literally make an accounting to the

---

[34]Spencer W. Kimball, Regional Representatives Seminar, April 3, 1975.

Lord by reporting to the Lord regarding your performance. Obviously, you should be accounting to yourself mentally and in writing regarding your performance. In some instances, you will account to those who preside over you.

> When performance is measured, performance improves. When performance is measured and reported, the rate of improvement accelerates.[35]

Step 3: Revise Your Goals Under Inspiration—In some cases you will find that goals you have set for yourself are too modest. For example, a missionary may set a goal to memorize 30 lines a day from the discussions during the early part of his mission, which would be a very defensible goal. Yet, a week or so later, as his level of dedication increases, this goal may prove to be very inadequate, according to his increased ability to memorize. Likewise, the goal of a missionary to baptize one person per month may be realistic in the early months of his mission. However, this same goal could, and would, prove to be far short of his capabilities later on in his mission. As a general rule of thumb, you should assume that your ability to perform will improve over time.

Unfortunately, some people are more conscientious during the early part of a particular endeavor such as a new calling in a ward. Once they become acquainted with the routine of that particular calling, they no longer approach the calling with the same conscientious attitude as they did initially.

> Every man is a diary in which he writes one story while intending to write another. His humblest moment is when he compares the two.[36]

When you are consistently able to achieve righteous desires that require the Lord's help, you are using faith as a principle of power. You can measure your faith by the number of predetermined righteous desires you accomplish over a period of time.

---

[35] Thomas S. Monson
[36] Hugh B. Brown

When you are first striving to exercise faith you should gauge success by progress as well as attainment. For example, if a missionary is presently able to memorize 30 lines of the missionary discussions a day, has set a goal to memorize 50 lines a day, and memorizes 40 lines the first day after he sets the goal, he has started to see the power of faith and should recognize it as such.

The first time you read this book answer the following question on a piece of paper.

How can you measure your faith?

If possible, discuss your answer with someone else who is reading this book.

Each time you reread this book:

Ask yourself:

How many predetermined righteous desires did you accomplish in the last year? In the last 30 days?

Express Gratitude

As you begin to experience the power of faith in your everyday life, it is very important to learn to express gratitude to your Father in Heaven.

Ingratitude is a crime more despicable than revenge.[37]

...ye must give thanks unto God in the Spirit for whatsoever blessing ye are blessed with. (D&C 46:32.)

Thou shalt thank the Lord thy God in all things. (D&C 59:7.)

There are two things you can train yourself to do on a daily basis that will help you catch and maintain the true spirit of gratitude. First train yourself to ponder and reflect on your many blessings, God's mercy, etc.; but more specifically, consider those things that you have been able to accomplish

---

[37] William G. Jordan, quoted by Heber J. Grant, *An Elder's Journal*, 3:298, April 15, 1906.

with the Lord's help. Secondly, you must work at recognizing the manifestations of the powers of heaven throughout each day.

> And in nothing doth man offend God, or against none is his wrath kindled, save those who confess not his hand in all things, and obey not his commandments. (D&C 59:21.)

You should train yourself to discern and recognize the powers of heaven. Each time you see the powers of heaven evidenced in any aspect of your life, make it a point to express specific gratitude to the Lord for the ways he has helped you during the day.

You should attempt to do this throughout the day, but most importantly, at the end of each day take a few minutes and reflect upon the day and identify specific instances where the powers of heaven were manifest in some way. In addition, attempt to critique yourself to ascertain things that you have said or done that have distracted from your faith and to what degree you have maintained an attitude of faith with respect to your righteous desires. Make it a policy to do this on a regular basis.

If you consistently take time to meditate and reflect on your blessings and to express specific gratitude to the Lord, your sensitivity to the Spirit will increase. As you draw closer to the Spirit, you will find your receptiveness to inspiration will become especially keen.

> A person may profit by noticing the first intimation of the spirit of revelation; for instance, when you feel pure intelligence flowing into you, it may give you sudden strokes of ideas, so that by noticing it, you may find it fulfilled the same day or soon; (i.e.) those things that were presented unto your mind by the Spirit of God, will come to pass; and thus by learning the Spirit of God and understanding it, you may grow into the principle of revelation, until you become perfect in Christ Jesus.[38]

As you are successful in cultivating a keen awareness of

---

[38] Joseph Smith, *Teachings of the Prophet Joseph Smith*, op. cit., p. 151.

the manifestations of the spirit, your ability to use faith as a principle of power will increase.

Record Your Experiences

Throughout your life, as you have experiences involving faith as a principle of power, record them and make them a meaningful part of your personal history. When you record faith-promoting experiences, be sure you describe in detail the process you went through in exercising faith as well as the result of your faith. Too often in writing about faith-promoting experiences the writer only talks about the blessing realized as a result of faith and fails to talk about his strivings, prayers, etc. required to receive the blessing.

Chapter Six

Develop A Deeper Understanding of Faith

Check Your Understanding

The following statements by Joseph Smith were quoted in chapter one of this book. Analyze them now in light of what you have read. If possible, discuss them with someone else who is reading this book.

1. "...as faith is the moving cause of all action in temporal concerns, so it is in spiritual;...

2. "...faith is not only the principle of action, but of power also,...

3. "Faith, then, is the first great governing principle which has power, dominion, and authority over all things."[39]

As you come to understand the power that is at your disposal through faith, you will find you can call down the powers of heaven to assist you in all your dealings and endeavors, not only your Church responsibilities. You should be just as inclined to look to the powers of heaven to assist you in

---

[39] Joseph Smith, *Lectures on Faith*, op. cit., pp. 8 & 10.

your profession or vocation as you would be to request this assistance in carrying out your duties in the Church. This is one of the great lessons of the Book of Mormon: if people seek the Lord's help in faith, He will assist them in all their affairs.

It is important for you to realize that the Lord's desire to assist you if your faith is sufficient to let him, is not restricted to church-related activities. You must realize that the Lord is just as inclined to assist you in your social life as He is in church callings. Through faith all your attributes, abilities, and social skills can be magnified (e.g., your ability to reason, your ability to understand what you read, your musical abilities, your ability to relate with other people, etc.).

> An intelligent being, in the image of God, possesses every organ, attribute, sense, sympathy, affection, of will, wisdom, love, power and gift, which is possessed by God himself. But... these attributes are in embryo, and are to be gradually developed.... The gift of the Holy Spirit adapts itself to all these organs or attributes. It quickens all the intellectual faculties, increases, enlarges, expands, and purifies all the natural passions and affections, and adapts them by the gift of wisdom to their lawful use. It inspires, develops, cultivates, and matures all the fine-toned sympathies, joys, tastes, kindred feelings, and affections of our nature. It inspires virtue, kindness, goodness, tenderness, gentleness, and charity. It develops beauty of person, form and features. It tends to health, vigor, animation, and social feeling. It develops and invigorates all the faculties of the physical and intellectual man.[40]

Many things you desire in life can be accomplished to a great extent by the faith that motivates you to make resolves and apply yourself in achieving them (e.g. improving your physical condition by jogging twelve miles a week, improving the relationship with a child by spending a half hour with the child each week). But in many instances, your desires will not be realized unless you learn to draw on the powers of heaven.

---

[40]Parley P. Pratt, quoted by James E. Talmage in *A Study of the Articles of Faith* (S.L.C.: The Church of Jesus Christ of Latter-day Saints, 1964), p. 487.

Learning to Recognize the Role of Faith

As you read the following episodes, identify those actions that are motivated by faith and the different ways the powers of heaven are evidenced as a result of faith as a principle of power.

Episode #1

A missionary laboring in a coal mining region near the town of Akron, Ohio, reported that a woman requested baptism in the middle of the winter during a snowstorm. The missionaries had no access to a baptismal font so it was necessary to baptize the woman in a little brook which ran through one of the member's lots. It was February and the weather was extremely cold. The missionary reported that when he stepped into the icy stream a pain shot up into his heart and he feared for a moment that he would step out again. He also began to fear that the woman would not be able to endure the cold. He prayed silently that the water would be tempered. He reported that there was a change in the water immediately for he felt no more cold, nor did the woman complain at all about the cold water.

Episode #2

Mary Jones had been active in extracurricular activities such as debate, drill team, etc., all through high school and had some dating opportunities. Upon graduating from high school she started attending BYU. She found she was everyone's friend but had very few dating opportunities, and when she did date, the young men would seldom ask her again. Even though she was very sociable, she was always a little tense in a dating relationship and was not able to relax and really be herself. She finally turned to her Father in Heaven and began to pray earnestly that the Lord would bless her that she would be able to relax in the dating relationship and that she would be able to help the fellow feel at ease. Within a few weeks she found that she was able to be much more relaxed on a date; her ability to be herself and to carry on a meaningful conversation improved a great deal. Once this happened, she found that the fellows were inclined to ask her out again and her opportunities for dating were much greater. Within a year she started to date the young man she ultimatly married.

Episode #3

On the 20th of the month, two missionaries were asked by their mission president how many baptisms they would have by the end of the month. The missionaries had two young couples scheduled to be baptized the following week, so they reported they would have four baptisms. Within two days, things came up that made it necessary to reschedule the baptism of the two couples to the following month. However, because of the commitment they had made, they went to their Father in Heaven and asked Him to prepare the way so that four people could be baptized by the end of the month. Then they proceeded to make this desire their primary focus as they worked harder than they had been working previously. By the last week of the month, one couple the missionaries had taught several weeks previously was baptized and another couple who had not been scheduled to be baptized when the elders made the commitment to their mission president was also baptized.

Episode #4

After several weeks of earnest inquiry and prayer, a young man decided that a particular graduate program at a major university was the graduate program he wanted to pursue. By this time, however, it was two months past the deadline for admission to the university so he turned to his Father in Heaven in prayer. He prayed that the way would be opened whereby even at this late date, he would be admitted to that particular graduate program. Once he established communication with the university, he prayed further that the hearts of those reviewing his credentials would be touched and they would be favorably impressed with his credentials and make the recommendation that the admissions deadline be waived in his case. He also prayed that he would be inspired in what he included in the applications he submitted to the university as well as in what he would say in his phone conversations and other correspondence with those who would be making the decision at the university. The desire to be admitted to this particular university became the primary focus of this young man's prayers and various days were designated for fasting in his effort to solicit the support of his Father in Heaven in this particular endeavor. Within a matter of three weeks, he received word that he had been admitted to the university.

Episode #5

A father of six contracted rheumatic fever and was confined to the hospital. When he was visited by his home teachers he asked them to give him a special blessing so that he could be healed from his sickness. He went on to explain that he had no education and the only work he was able to perform was manual labor and it would be essential that he be restored to his full health and strength so that he could return to manual labor in order to support his family.

The home teachers proceeded to administer to the man. Upon returning in a week, they were informed by the man that his prognosis was still the same—his heart was severly impaired and the doctors had indicated that he would not be able to return to manual labor. The senior home teacher became perplexed in that the blessing was not realized. He turned to his Father in Heaven in secret prayer, desiring to know why this blessing had not been realized. It was revealed to his mind that his mind had become very preoccupied with the other demands in his life—his schooling, job, etc., and that if this blessing was to be realized, he would have to make this desire a matter of focus in his daily prayers as well as during other times during the day.

He returned to the hospital and anointed and blessed the man again through the power of the priesthood, with the resolve that the desire to see the man healed would become a very specific preoccupation of his mind and very integral to his daily prayers. Upon returning to the hospital the following week, the man announced that his current tests revealed that his heart no longer evidenced any damage from the illness, and there was every indication that he would be restored to his full health and would be able to support his family.

Episode #6

A young couple had two sons, the eldest of which was five years old. This child began to evidence a very serious behavioral problem. Where he had previously been very outgoing, enthusiastic, and cheerful, he was now sullen, withdrawn, and introspective. The young father was pursuing a degree in psychology. He immediately began to turn to his various textbooks for help in coping with his son's behavioral problems. Unable to find any explanation in his textbooks, he turned to his professors, hoping they would be able to provide him some counsel as to how to cope with the problem.

Finally, the young father turned to his Father in Heaven in prayer, and in the attitude of a fast, prayed earnestly that he would be inspired regarding the problem. It was revealed to the young father's mind that his eldest son was entitled to the distinction of the eldest. The father immediately realized that it had been his policy to involve both sons in all activities, and when he would buy something for one son, he would always buy the same thing for the other. Following this inspiration, he began to identify specific things that he could do to designate the older son as the eldest and make it clear to the eldest son that he was entitled to do certain things or have certain types of clothes, etc. as a result of the fact that he was the eldest. Immediately the behavioral problem that had been manifest was alleviated.

Episode #7

"Shortly [after] our branch became a ward,... I became the bishop. At a stake meeting one of the bishops told how he had devoted an hour each day to prayer during the previous week. So moving was his spirit, so great his experience, that my soul desired this same joy. I vowed to myself that the next day would find me in an hour of prayer for myself, my family, my ward, and my job. But the next day was Sunday, and bishopric meeting was at 6 A.M. To arise early enough, I would have to get up at 4 A.M. My resolve vanished in sleep and fled to the corner of unfulfilled promises.

"With my resolve renewed by a successful Sabbath, I set the alarm for Monday morning. As it rang, I sat up, put my feet on the floor and attempted to rise. At once, and with great force, I was grabbed about the shoulders by a king-size mattress that pulled me forcibly back into its warmth and softness. I struggled valiantly for perhaps five or six seconds before I succumbed to its invitation. Then I gave up and slumbered on. . . .

"[Later] I thought, 'How can I be a bishop of a ward if the members are praying harder than I am? How can I be a spiritual guide for them?'

"The next morning found me in a small wooded area next to our home, where I poured out my heart to the Lord and meditated. Nearly an hour went by. The rewards were gratifying. As I prayed and talked and listened, a calmness of spirit and an inner warmth permeated my whole being, and my soul rejoiced. There were no heavenly messengers, no great lights, no visions or voices, but I felt myself lifted to new spiritual levels in that hour, and I knew I would never again be satisfied with a lesser effort in prayer.

"Eventually, I retired to the meetinghouse each morning and there, with a chapter or two of the scriptures to stimulate my thinking to some serious meditation, I found myself pondering the things of the Spirit until I felt that I was ready to speak to my Father. Gradually, almost imperceptibly, I experienced the revelatory process Joseph Smith described, as strokes of pure intelligence entered my mind. Ideas for ward organization, solutions to family problems, new concepts for my seminary and institute classes, and a deep personal strength emerged daily and profusely from these prayers. I soon found a pen and pad of paper were necessary to write down the ideas as they came. The promptings proved valuable as we reorganized our ward auxiliaries and issued call after call to people who knew of their new callings before they were made.

"My family also benefited as their husband and father in the home, a priesthood bearer, gave more inspired direction and counsel. Feelings of love and peace increased, and we rejoiced in new spiritual strength. My institute and seminary classes became more vibrant and interesting as I could see myself teaching more and more by the Spirit. The scriptures began to open up as never before, and I actually understood for the first time some of the writings of Isaiah that Jesus had told the Nephites were so valuable. (See 3 Ne. 23:1-5.)"[41]

Episode #8

"The pressures of my job as sales manager for a home building company can be very acute at times. I had been a member of the Church for about six months when two problems confronted me one morning, each within about five minutes of the other. First, one of the salesmen rejected an offer to join with the rest of the sales team for a lunch given by the company. I was hurt because we were a close-knit, friendly team.

"As I sat miserably in my office, contemplating the problem, the company manager came in to remind me that we had about a half million dollars worth of new homes that had been unsold for a year. He wanted me to make a positive effort, work miracles if necessary, to get them sold.

"Heavy with the weight of these two problems, I picked up my jacket as soon as he left and walked out to the car. I drove to one of the offending houses, unlocked it, went inside,

[41] Richard D. Anthony, "I Was a Bishop before I Really Learned to Pray," *The Ensign*, January 1976, p. 52-53.

and locked the door behind me. I walked up the stairs, and in the empty lounge I knelt to pray. At that moment something unusual happened. Before I could even think the words that I wanted to say to my Heavenly Father, in a beautiful clear light within my closed eyes I seemed to see my problem salesman happily accepting the challenge to sell all those difficult homes; he also agreed not to be permitted to sell easier ones until the others were sold. He would be given a completely free hand to organize his own campaign, promotions, advertising, and his own time. He would be rewarded by a higher rate of commission.

"Within two months those homes that a previous salesman had had so much trouble with were sold by my problem salesman. He was a changed man after his successful response to a big challenge, and the manager was delighted.

"I am grateful that the Lord blessed me with that brief experience in that upstairs room and showed me the wonders of his ways. I have known ever since that he listens to our prayers and guides us through the eternal plans for his children."[42]

Episode #9

A young man accepted a job at a resort during the summer following his junior year in high school. Upon arriving at the resort the manager called him into his office and related some of the problems they were having with the young people working at the resort involving primarily sex and drinking. He expressed the hope that the young man would attempt to avoid similar problems. The young man left the discussion very sobered; he had never lived away from home previously and he had been raised in an LDS community. With a real sense of concern that he would be able to keep himself removed from the sins he would be confronted with, he went to his Heavenly Father and sought his help. In the course of

---

[42] Roy B. Webb, "Businessman's Prayer in an Upper Room," *The Ensign*, January 1976, pp. 50–51.

the summer the young man sensed his prayers were answered in many ways. He found he was able to explain his reasons for not smoking and drinking without being apologetic, and the other kids were very understanding. Through the power of discernment he was able to avoid evil on several occasions. For example, one night at a party he danced with a young lady and really found her enjoyable to talk to. However, he had a distinct impression not to accept her invitation to attend another party with her. He later learned the young lady had only wanted to seduce him, as Potiphar's wife did Joseph. (Gen. 39:7-12.) On another occasion he had a distinct impression to avoid any association with a particular fellow. A week later the fellow was picked up on homosexual charges.

Episode #10

"On my first visit to the fabled village of Sauniatu, so loved by President McKay, my wife and I met with a large gathering of small children. At the conclusion of our messages to these shy, yet beautiful, youngsters, I suggested to the native Samoan teacher that we go forward with the closing exercises. As he announced the final hymn, I suddenly felt compelled to personally greet each of these 247 children. My watch revealed that the time was too short for such a privilege, so I discounted the impression. Before the benediction was to be spoken, I again felt this strong impression to shake the hand of each child. This time I made the desire known to the instructor, who displayed a broad and beautiful Samoan smile. He spoke in Samoan to the children, and they beamed their approval of his comments.

"The instructor then revealed to me the reason for his and their joy. He said, 'When we learned that President McKay had assigned a member of the Council of the Twelve to visit us in far-away Samoa, I told the children if they would each one earnestly and sincerely pray and exert faith like the Bible accounts of old, that the Apostle would visit our tiny village at Sauniatu, and through their faith, he would be impressed to greet each child with a personal handclasp.' Tears could not be restrained as each of those precious boys and girls walked shyly by and whispered softly to us a sweet *talofa lava*. The gift of faith had been evidenced."[43]

Episode #11

"I should like to give you in conclusion an experience that came to my attention two days after the passing of that great prophet of God, Elder Matthew Cowley. It was given to me by a man who some thirty-five or forty years before had been district president of Brother Cowley down in New Zealand as he labored with those Maori people. He had only been out for two and one half months, and a district missionary conference was called. In one of those sessions, the morning session, Brother Cowley had an opportunity to speak. As the story has been related to me, he spoke for fifteen or twenty minutes in a fluent Maori tongue, so much so that it amazed the older Maori people in the congregation.

"After the meeting, the district president and Brother Cowley were walking to a Maori home to partake of food between the sessions, and the district president said, 'How did you do it?' Brother Cowley asked, 'Do what?' 'How did you master this Maori language in such a short time?' A young missionary, seventeen years of age!

"Brother Cowley said, 'When I came here I did not know one word of Maori, but I decided I was going to learn twenty new words each day, and I did. But when I came to put them together, I was not successful.' By this time they were passing a cornfield, and Brother Cowley said, 'You see that cornfield? I went out there, and I talked to the Lord, but before that, I fasted, and that night I tried again, but the words just didn't seem to jell. So the next day I fasted again, and I went out into that cornfield, and I talked to the Lord. Again I tried that night with a little more success. On the third day I fasted again, and I went out into the cornfield, and I talked to the

---

[43] Thomas S. Monson, *Conference Report*, October 1966, pp. 9-10; see also "God's Gifts to Polynesia's People," *The Improvement Era*, December 1966, pp. 1101-1102.

Lord. I told the Lord that I believed his Church and kingdom had been established upon the earth; that men had the authority to proclaim the fulness of the gospel of Jesus Christ which pertained to the salvation and exaltation of our Heavenly Father's children. I told him that I had been called by this same authority to fill a mission, but if this was not the mission in which I was to serve to please make it known because I wanted to serve where I could accomplish the greatest amount of good.'

"That was the spirit of Brother Cowley. He said, 'The next morning, as we knelt in family prayer in the Maori home, I was called upon by the head of the household to be mouth. I tried to speak in English, and I could not. When I tried in Maori, the words just flowed forth, and I knew that God had answered my prayer and this was where I should serve.' A young lad seventeen years of age!"[44]

Episode #12

A little boy had a dog that he dearly loved. As the dog began to age, he finally reached a point that he could hardly walk and began to lose his sight. The dog could only eat things that were cooked and cut into small pieces. He finally reached a point that he was not eating much of anything and it was evident that he would die. The little boy's father finally decided that it would be in the dog's best interest to take him into the woods and shoot him. The little boy understood that his father was not a bad man and that his intent was to put the old dog out of his misery. The father had made an effort to help the boy to see that it would be in the dog's best interest to be shot. The father had explained that it was very difficult for him to make the decision, because he liked the old dog too, and the dog had become a member of the family. He explained to the boy that he had realized for some time that it was the thing that should be done but that he had continually

---

[44] John Longden, *Conference Report*, April 1955, p. 59; see also "Prayer Makes the Difference," *The Improvement Era*, June 1955, pp. 412-413.

put it off. Trying to be as understanding as he could, the little boy made the request that he be given one more opportunity to try to get the dog to eat and regain wome of his strength. The father consented to the boy's request.

The little boy began to go to great pains to prepare special food and would even attempt to feed the dog by hand. In spite of his efforts, the dog still was unable to eat. The little boy would put the dog in his wagon and pull him around, trying to get the dog to show some excitement again about some of their favorite places and things. And yet the old dog was just too sick to show any interest in those things that had previously provided both the boy and the dog such happiness. By the end of the second day the little boy began to see that his effort was hopeless, and he was sick at heart as he thought of the bullet penetrating his dog and his dog bleeding and twitching as he would finally die.

It was at this moment that the little boy decided to turn to his Father in Heaven for help. He retired to his room and knelt down by his bed and began to pray to his Father in Heaven. His request was very simple. It was his prayer that Heavenly Father would let his old dog die so that it would not be necessary for his father to shoot him. He explained the situation to his Father in Heaven as to why it had become necessary for the dog to to be shot and explained his simple case that he felt that it would be better if the dog could just die and not have to be shot. The little boy was realistic and went on to explain that his dog was not necessarily a special dog although he certainly meant a lot to him. He recognized the dog's failings as far as having bitten the milkman on two occasions, but he was quick to go on and explain that generally the dog did obey, and before be got sick, he was able to do many tricks and would fetch sticks and balls when the little boy would throw them. He went on to explain to his Father in Heaven that the old dog was no longer able to enjoy the things that they used to enjoy together and that the old dog had finally reached a point where he was virtually unable to get around at all. The little boy concluded by saying if Heavenly Father would let his dog die in a nice, easy, natural way, he promised that he would be especially grateful to his Father in Heaven for responding to his request.

As the little boy left his bedroom and was going down the steps, he met his father. His father said he was just coming up to tell him it would not be necessary to shoot his dog after all—his dog had just died.

Episode #13

"On the third of October, in the year nineteen hundred and eighteen, I sat in my room pondering over the scriptures;

"And reflecting upon the great atoning sacrifice that was made by the Son of God, for the redemption of the world;

"And the great and wonderful love made manifest by the Father and the Son in the coming of the Redeemer into the world;

"That through his atonement, and by obedience to the principles of the gospel, mankind might be saved.

"While I was thus engaged, my mind reverted to the writings of the apostle Peter, to the primitive saints scattered abroad throughout Pontus, Galatia, Cappadocia, and other parts of Asia, where the gospel had been preached after the crucifixion of the Lord.

"I opened the Bible and read the third and fourth chapters of the first epistle of Peter, and as I read I was greatly impressed, more than I had ever been before, with the following passages:

" 'For Christ also hath once suffered for sins, the just for the unjust, that he might bring us to God, being put to death in the flesh, but quickened by the Spirit:

" 'By which also he went and preached unto the spirits in prison;

" 'Which sometime were disobedient, when once the long-suffering of God waited in the days of Noah, while the ark was a preparing, wherein few, that is, eight souls were saved by water. (1 Peter 3:18-20.)

" 'For, for this cause was the gospel preached also to them that are dead, that they might be judged according to men in the flesh, but live according to God in the spirit.' (1 Peter 4:6.)

"As I pondered over these things which are written, the eyes of my understanding were opened, and the Spirit of the Lord rested upon me, and I saw the hosts of the dead, both small and great.

"And there were gathered together in one place an innumerable company of the spirits of the just, who had been faithful in the testimony of Jesus while they lived in mortality;

"And who had offered sacrifice in the similitude of the great sacrifice of the Son of God, and had suffered tribulation in their Redeemer's name.

"All these had departed the mortal life, firm in the hope of glorious resurrection, through the grace of God the Father and his Only Begotten Son, Jesus Christ.

"I beheld that they were filled with joy and gladness, and were rejoicing together because the day of their deliverance was at hand.

"They were assembled awaiting the advent of the Son of God into the spirit world, to declare their redemption from the bands of death.

"Their sleeping dust was to be restored unto its perfect frame, bone to his bone, and the sinews and the flesh upon them, the spirit and the body to be united never again to be divided, that they might receive a fulness of joy.

"While this vast multitude waited and conversed, rejoicing in the hour of their deliverance from the chains of death, the Son of God appeared, declaring liberty to the captives who had been faithful;

"And there he preached to them the everlasting gospel, the doctrine of the resurrection and the redemption of mankind from the fall, and from individual sins on conditions of repentance.

"But unto the wicked he did not go, and among the ungodly and the unrepentant who had defiled themselves while in the flesh, his voice was not raised;

"Neither did the rebellious who rejected the testimonies and the warnings of the ancient prophets behold his presence, nor look upon his face.

"Where these were, darkness reigned, but among the righteous there was peace;

"And the saints rejoiced in their redemption, and bowed the knee and acknowledged the Son of God as their Redeemer and Deliverer from death and the chains of hell.

"Their countenances shone and the radiance from the presence of the Lord rested upon them, and they sang praises unto his holy name.

"I marveled, for I understood that the Savior spent about three years in his ministry among the Jews and those of the house of Israel, endeavoring to teach them the everlasting gospel and call them unto repentance;

"And yet, notwithstanding his mighty works, and miracles, and proclamation of the truth, in great power and authority, there were but few who hearkened to his voice, and rejoiced in his presence, and received salvation at his hands.

"But his ministry among those who were dead was limited to the brief time intervening between the crucifixion and his resurrection;

"And I wondered at the words of Peter—wherein he said that the Son of God preached unto the spirits in prison, who sometime were disobedient, when once the long-suffering of God waited in the days of Noah—and how it was possible for him to preach to those spirits and perform the necessary labor among them in so short a time.

"And as I wondered, my eyes were opened, and my understanding quickened, and I perceived that the Lord went not in person among the wicked and the disobedient who had rejected the truth, to teach them;

"But behold, from among the righteous, he organized his forces and appointed messengers, clothed with power and authority, and commissioned them to go forth and carry the light of the gospel to them that were in darkness, even to all the spirits of men; and thus was the gospel preached to the dead.

"And the chosen messengers went forth to declare the acceptable day of the Lord, and proclaim liberty to the captives who were bound, even unto all who would repent of their sins and receive the gospel.

"Thus was the gospel preached to those who had died in their sins, without a knowledge of the truth, or in transgression, having rejected the prophets.

"These were taught faith in God, repentance from sin, vicarious baptism for the remission of sins, the gift of the Holy Ghost by the laying on of hands,

"And all other principles of the gospel that were necessary for them to know in order to qualify themselves that they might be judged according to men in the flesh, but live according to God in the spirit.

"And so it was made known among the dead, both small and great, the unrighteous as well as the faithful, that redemption had been wrought through the sacrifice of the Son of God upon the cross.

"Thus was it made known that our Redeemer spent his time during his sojourn in the world of spirits, instructing and preparing the faithful spirits of the prophets who had testified of him in the flesh;

"That they might carry the message of redemption unto all the dead, unto whom he could not go personally, because of their rebellion and transgression, that they through the ministration of his servants might also hear his words.

"Among the great and mighty ones who were assembled in this vast congregation of the righteous were Father Adam, the Ancient of Days and father of all,

"And our glorious Mother Eve, with many of her faithful daughters who had lived through the ages and worshiped the true and living God.

"Abel, the first martyr, was there, and his brother Seth, one of the mighty ones, who was in the express image of his father, Adam.

"Noah, who gave warning of the flood; Shem, the great high priest; Abraham, the father of the faithful; Isaac, Jacob, and Moses, the great law-giver of Israel;

"And Isaiah, who declared by prophecy that the Redeemer was anointed to bind up the broken-hearted, to proclaim liberty to the captives, and the opening of the prison to them that were bound, were also there."[45]

Scriptures on Faith

The first time you read this book, read Alma 32:26-29 and, if possible, discuss the meaning of the scripture with someone else who is reading this book, then read and discuss the following adaptation of Alma 32:26-29.

> Now, as I said concerning faith, it is not a perfect knowledge, and so it is with your righteous desires. You cannot know of your ability to accomplish them at first, unto perfection, any more than faith is a perfect knowledge. But behold, if ye will awake and arouse your faculties, even to an experimentation upon your ability to achieve your righteous desires with my help, and exercise a particle of faith — even if ye can do no more than desire to achieve — let this desire work within you, even until you are willing to give place in your mind to think consistently about your righteous desire. Now we will compare

---

[45] *The Pearl of Great Price*, Joseph F. Smith—Vision of the Redemption of the Dead, verses 1-42.

this desire unto a seed, and if you do not cast it out by your unbelief, that you will resist the Spirit of the Lord, behold, it will begin to swell within your breast, and when you feel this swelling motion you will begin to say within yourself, I can achieve it or I begin to have confidence in my ability to achieve it, for I beginneth to see how it is attainable. Now behold, would not this increase your faith? I say unto you, yea.

The first time you read this book read Ether 12:6 and, if possible, discuss the meaning of the scripture with someone else who is reading this book, then read and discuss the following adaptation of Ether 12:6.

Faith is things which are hoped for (righteous desires) and not seen (you cannot see on the basis of your own ability and circumstances how these desires can be realized); wherefore, dispute not because ye see not, for ye receive no witness (assurance from the Lord that He will open the way for your desires to be realized) until after the trial of your faith (exercising faith for a sustained period of time).

Each time your reread this book, read the following scriptures aloud and discuss them with someone else who is reading this book.

Matthew 21:22	Mosiah 27:14
D&C 11:10, 14, 17	Alma 41:3-7
D&C 18:19	Alma 57:25-27
D&C 26:2	3 Nephi 7:18
D&C 29:6-7	Mormon 1:13-14
D&C 44:2	Mormon 2:26
D&C 60:7	Ether 12
D&C 66:8	Moroni 7:37
D&C 130:20-21	Moroni 10:7-18
John 15:1-8	Psalms 37:4-6

In addition, each time you reread this book, read several of the episodes from the Book of Mormon listed below. Analyze the role of faith in each of the episodes. Note especially the various powers of heaven that are manifest and the different circumstances when the powers of heaven assist mortal men.

1 Nephi 1:5-19, 2:1-4	3 Nephi 3:9-25
1 Nephi 2:16-20	3 Nephi 4:1-12, 24-33
1 Nephi 3:2-31, 4:1-27	3 Nephi 7:15-22

1 Nephi 7:1-22	3 Nephi 17:5-8; 20
1 Nephi 11:1-6	3 Nephi 17:21-24
1 Nephi 16:18-31	3 Nephi 19:35-36
1 Nephi 17:7-55, 18:1-3	4 Nephi 29 through 33
1 Nephi 18:9-22	Mormon 1:13-17
Jacob 7:1-22	Mormon 3:7-16
Enos	Mormon 8:10-11
Words of Mormon 13:14	Mormon 9:15-27
Mosiah 7:1-33; 22:1-16	Ether 1 through 3
Mosiah 23:25-39; 24:1-25	Ether 6:1-17
Mosiah 27:1-37	Ether 12:1-41
Alma 2:1-36	Moroni 7:33-48
Alma 14:1-29	Moroni 8:22-29
Alma 15:1-12	Moroni 9:1-6
Alma 16:1-8	Moroni 10:1-25
Alma 17 through 36	Helaman 4:1-26
Alma 43:4-54; 44:1-20	Helaman 5:1-51
Alma 46:1-37	Helaman 6:1-6
Alma 48:1-17; 49:1-28	Helaman 7 through 12

Finally, as you read the scriptures in general, look for instances where the powers of heaven are manifest as a result of personal faith.

Make A Systematic Review

Frequently evaluate your ability to establish and achieve goals (righteous desires) by asking yourself the following questions:

1. Do I consistently follow President Kimball's admonition to set goals?
2. When I set goals that cannot be attained without the Lord's help, do I consistently remind myself of the role of faith in calling down the powers of heaven?
3. Do I keep the following points in mind when I formulate my goals:
   a. Are my goals realistic?

   b. Do I focus on a few pertinent goals at one time rather than attempting to focus on many goals simultaneously?

   c. Are my goals challenging?

   d. In the formulation of some goals, do I seek counsel from others regarding what would be realistic expectation under the circumstances?

   e. Do I set both long range and short term goals?

   f. Are my goals based on proper motives and in accord with the Lord's will?

4. Am I willing to promise my Father in Heaven that I will live more righteously?

5. Do I weigh priorities wisely as I set goals?

6. Do I stay close to the spirit of my Heavenly Father to avoid becoming discouraged?

7. Do I keep a consistent and accurate accounting of my performance in achieving goals by:

   a. Reducing my goals to writing?

   b. Measuring my performance against my predetermined goals on a regular basis?

   c. Revising my goals under inspiration?

8. Do I use each goal as a means and not an end (e.g., Does the achievement of my goals cause me to work even more diligently)?

9. Do I make a consistent effort to focus my thoughts on my goals?

10. Do I consistently exert myself mentally regarding my goals (righteous desires)?

11. Have I been successful in enduring my trials of faith?

Because of the nature of the topic this book deals with, you will not be able to grasp the concepts by reading the book once. If you decide you want to make the powers that come through faith an integral part of your life, you should resolve to reread this book at least once a week for eight consecutive weeks; then at least once a month thereafter. Each time you reread this book, you should read the designated scriptures and respond to the questions.

About the Author

Grant Von Harrison is a native of Cedar City, Utah. He received his B.A. degree from Brigham Young University in 1962; his M.A. from Adams State College in 1965; and his doctorate in Instructional Science from UCLA in 1969.

Dr. Harrison taught for the Church Educational System for seven years. He worked as a project associate and consultant for the Institute for Educational Development and was a human factors analyst with System Development Corporation.

Since joining the Brigham Young University faculty in 1969, he has developed numerous instructional programs. He is the author of the books *Drawing on the Powers of Heaven* and *Tools for Missionaries*. He is the author and developer of the structured tutoring model which has provided the basis for literacy programs the Church is using in South America; he has also developed and authored various instructional materials designed to be used by nonprofessionals to teach reading, mathematics, and foreign languages.

Dr. Harrison is an active member of the Church of Jesus Christ of Latter-day Saints. Much of his church service has been associated with missionary work, having served as a full-time missionary and in three mission presidencies. He served as the Director of Instruction in the former Mission Home in Salt Lake City and also as a Branch President at the Missionary Training Center in Provo, Utah. He has taught the Missionary Preparation class at Brigham Young University and also in his home ward. He is presently serving as the Teacher's Quorum Advisor in his home ward in Orem, Utah.